WHAT THE HELL JUST HAPPENED?

Tamara Miller

ISBN 978-1-956696-93-6 (paperback)
ISBN 978-1-956696-94-3 (hardcover)
ISBN 978-1-956696-95-0 (digital)

Copyright © 2021 by Tamara Miller

All rights reserved. No part of this publication may be reproduced, distributed, or transmitted in any form or by any means, including photocopying, recording, or other electronic or mechanical methods without the prior written permission of the publisher. For permission requests, solicit the publisher via the address below.

This book is a work of non-fiction.

Rushmore Press LLC
1 800 460 9188
www.rushmorepress.com

Printed in the United States of America

DEDICATION

*To Pep and Heather Davis who
were there for me during my darkest hour.*

ONE

"Randall! Randall!" I yelled. "Don't do this!" *Is he having a heart attack?* I wondered. *His face is so red. Get a wet cloth and put it on his forehead.* I ran to the kitchen, grabbed a washcloth and ran cold water on it, and ran back to his chair, placing the cloth on his head.

"Randall! Randall! Can you hear me?" I shouted. *No, no, that's not right. Get something cold and place it on the back of his neck.* I ran to the refrigerator and grabbed a cold can of soda, ran back to him, and placed it on the back of his neck. His arms were drawn up to his chest and his hands were in tight fists.

"Honey, can you hear me?" I started to cry. *What to do? What should I do? Call 911?*

I dialed, and the operator answered and asked, "What is your emergency?"

"It's my husband!" I yelled in the phone. My voice was so shaky it's a wonder she understood me. "He looks like he's having a heart attack!" I couldn't stop crying. I patted his shoulder and said, "Honey I called 911 and they should be here soon. I wish I could know if you can hear me," as I talked to the operator at the same time. I gave her my address.

***

It was just going to be one of our normal four day trips to the desert. We have had a mobile home on the Colorado River for more than forty years. We were both retired. My husband, Randall, retired seventeen years ago after forty-two years as an engineer at Metropolitan Water District (MWD). I retired seven years ago from my job as an Executive Assistant at KB Home.

We went to the river about once a month, sometimes twice. It is always relaxing there for me, a perfect place to write and read. Randall loves to fish and usually has a project to work on. He always finds a reason to go into town where the Blue Water Casino is located.

The day before we left, I had some errands to run. "I'm going to the store to pick up a few things and then take the Grant Deed to the bank," I told him. That was the last item I had to do to complete our Living Trust. I had the document for over two weeks, but just hadn't got around to dropping it off.

"While you're out, stop by the bank and pick up some cash," he responded.

"Okay. See you in a little bit."

Three months ago we opened up a Living Trust. We travel to Mexico twice a year, and it bothered us that all we had was a will. Not that we are wealthy, but we attended a seminar and realized the need for a Living Trust to direct our assets properly, and express who should have what in writing, after we are gone.

When I returned home, Randall asked, "Did the bank ask anything about the trust?"

"No they just made a copy of it for their file. I'm going to put the original in our trust binder. We probably didn't even need to give it to them, because we only have two more payments on the house. I never thought we would see the day when it would be paid off."

"I know. We'll have to celebrate," said Randall.

The next morning, I packed the ice chest along with items for Kissy, my sweet little dog. She is a white Malti-Poo. We have had her for ten years. Randall was against having another dog, but they have become best friends.

WHAT THE HELL JUST HAPPENED?

"I'm going to gas up the truck," he said. "Be ready when I get back."

I just ignored that comment because that's what he always says. It didn't make any sense to me that we have to leave early in the morning, but I just go along with it. He's the driver, so he gets to make the rules.

Kissy and I are ready, and the car is loaded. We pulled out of the driveway at 8:05 a.m. It's a four-hour drive, during which I would have liked to talk to him about life and everything that was bugging me. He told me that wasn't going to happen. So it was a quiet drive. Who was I kidding? I knew he didn't want to listen to me talk for four hours.

Later into the ride, I asked, "Do you have any projects this trip?" He usually had something to work on. He never sat idle – unless NASCAR or a sports event was on television.

"No," he answered. "There's an off-road race in Parker I want to go to, and one night we'll go to dinner at the Casino." He looked at me with a smile.

"I hope you get lucky this time." About five years ago, he was a big winner. He kept thinking it would happen again. If not in Las Vegas, maybe at the Blue Water Casino.

As we arrived at our trailer at Windmill Resort, on the Parker strip, it was easy to spot our home because it was the only mobile that had a lawn, except for the ones on the front row at the water's edge. Like at home, Randall took pride in how our yard looked. Sometimes it would be 110 degrees outside, and the first thing he did was mow the grass. I was afraid he would have a stroke due to the heat, but there was nothing I could do to stop him.

We had a regular routine of things we each did when we first arrived. We unloaded the car together, and I would put our groceries away. Randall would sweep the leaves off our porch area. It was over 100 degrees, and I couldn't help saying, "I hope you aren't going to mow the yard."

"No," he answered. "I'm just going to water things down."

All the groceries were put away. Randall had already taken the patio furniture out of the shed, so I was wiping it off.

"I feel a little dizzy," he said, as he turned off the water and put down the hose. "I'm going inside and sit down."

I didn't think anything about it because of the heat. Besides it was time for the NASCAR trials on television. I soon heard the sound of cars buzzing around the track on the television in the living room. I finished cleaning the patio furniture and then went inside.

This was the beginning of madness! Randall was sitting on his recliner, his face was bright red, and his eyes were glazed. The first thing that entered my mind was that he had been stung by several horse flies, which had happened to him several years ago, and was having a reaction. Then I noticed his hands were in fists up against his chest. He didn't respond to me when I yelled his name.

At first I panicked. Then I told myself we'll get through this. If he was having a heart attack and with some medical assistance, and a little down time, life would return to normal. I had no idea how serious his condition was.

€

I didn't know this was the moment my life would change forever. I didn't know that I would never hear again all the things he said to me that I found annoying, like: "Hurry up, we're going to be late," or "Get out of the shower, you are using too much water." If I was too long when running errands, he always asked, "Where have you been. I thought you got lost." He always warned me, "Be careful backing out the car," as if it was the first time I'd backed out of the garage.

Because he gets up at five in the morning, he would ask, "Are you going to sleep all day?" Now I would give anything to hear him say those words again.

I didn't know this was the moment the things I took for granted that Randall did around the house and yard were now all my responsibility.

It hadn't entered my mind that suffering with the heartache of losing the love of my life I would be faced with rules, regulations, and overwhelming paperwork that accompanied a death.

I hope if this moment happens to you, you will find my story helpful.

TWO

I was yelling into the phone to the 911 operator out of frustration, and I was so scared. "Is anyone on the way?"

"We're sending an ambulance," said the operator. "You need to get your husband on the floor. He needs to be lying flat."

"I can't. He's in a chair and dead weight!" I yelled back.

"Pull him out of the chair by his feet"

"He'll hit his head if I do that."

"Don't worry about his head. Just get him on the floor." I could tell she was just as frustrated with me as I was with her.

"Okay. I'm going to put you on speaker phone." I laid the phone on the floor.

"Honey, can you hear me?" His eyes were still glazed, but he was breathing. In fact, periodically he took loud gasps.

All right. Here goes nothing, I thought. *If I have to get him on the floor, that's exactly what I'll do.*

I straddled him on the chair and put my arms under his. "Randall, I'm going to lift you and lay you on the floor. If there is any way you can help me that would be great." It's amazing what strength you have if you need it. I lifted him up, turned him away from the chair, and laid him on the floor.

"Okay, he's on the floor," I yelled at the phone.

"Do you know how to do chest compressions?" asked the 911 operator.

"Yes. I just saw it done on television the other night."

WHAT THE HELL JUST HAPPENED?

"Okay. We're going to do it together. I want you to do it while we count aloud to ten. Don't stop, just count to ten over and over again. Is he breathing?"

"Yes, and every once in awhile he takes loud gasps."

"All right, start the compressions, and tell me every time he takes a deep breath." And so we started.

"One, two … ten," I counted aloud along with the operator. About every third set of ten he would gasp for air. I was now sobbing as I counted.

"When will help get here?" I yelled into the phone.

"You're doing fine," said the operator.

"Is anyone coming yet?" I yelled as I counted.

"Yes, they are on the way."

"One, two … ten." It seemed like it was taking forever. I had no measure of time. Even looking back I can't tell you how long I continued the compressions.

"Where are they?" I yelled. "Are they close yet?"

"They should be there soon. Don't stop."

Our mobile home was on the California side of the river. I knew the closest ambulance was at the Indian Hospital in Parker, which was a good thirty to forty-five minutes away.

"Where are they?" I yelled again, in between sobs. I had no idea if Randall even knew what was going on. "I hear them! I hear them!" I yelled to the operator.

"Don't stop your compressions until the attendants are with you."

"I won't. One, two…ten." My voice was quivering as I sobbed. "Please Randall, don't leave me. Don't leave me," I said between counting.

"We're here now. We've got him," said one of the men as he took over the compressions.

One of the other men helped me up from the floor and walked me to my couch, where I collapsed.

"Don't worry," he said. "You did a fine job, we've got him now."

Watching three men work on my husband was surreal. One pumped his chest, a lot harder than I had. I wondered if I had done it hard enough. One man placed an oxygen mask on him, and the third man was doing something else, I couldn't tell what.

Kissy came out from behind the recliner. She was shaking. A dog's instinct told her something was wrong. I picked her up and held her tight. At this point, I don't know who was comforting whom.

One of the men asked me, "Can you go to the boat ramp? There is a rescue boat coming and you can tell them where we are."

I don't think I even answered him. I took Kissy and ran to the boat ramp. A boat was docking with two men in it. I started waving my arm and yelling, "Over here, over here," as I still held Kissy tightly under the other arm.

One man stayed in the boat while the other jumped out and followed me. It looked like he was caring a medical case.

It was very crowded with four men in my small kitchen area where Randall was lying. Also, a fireman arrived in case they needed any additional help.

Kissy and I sat on the couch and watched them still working on Randall. It didn't appear he was conscious. I couldn't stand to watch any longer, I wanted to talk to my family. I felt very alone.

I need to call the kids and let them know what is going on. The reception for cell phones was questionable, so I went outside and finally found a connection. I called my daughter, Mindy, at work, and of course I got her voicemail. Then I called my son, Cory, voicemail again. I tried my daughter again, voicemail. I lost it, and yelled into the phone, "Now would be a good time for someone to answer the phone!"

One of the men came outside and said, "We are going to take your husband to the hospital." I wanted to ask if he was going to be all right, but how could they know. Besides, I didn't want the answer.

There wasn't room in the ambulance for me. The fireman asked if I was able to drive. I started to answer yes, but I realized I was too upset. "Maybe not," I said.

"I'll take you," he offered.

"That would be great." I stood and watched them bring Randall out and put him in the ambulance. I can't explain the emotion I was feeling. It was like watching someone taking a piece of me away, and I couldn't stop them. I didn't know who to leave Kissy with so I locked her inside the mobile home. As I drove away with the fireman, I saw Kissy standing on her hind legs scratching at the glass door. What was she thinking? She looked as scared as I felt.

As we left the mobile home park, I decided to call Mindy's husband Darren. He's in sales, so I knew he would answer his phone or at least check his voicemail. I left a message, "I'm at the river. Tell Mindy something has happened to Dad, and they are taking him to the hospital. Call me on my cell." He called me right back, and I told him what was going on.

***

On the thirty-five minute drive to the hospital I made small talk, trying to keep from crying. "I can't believe this is happening," I chatted. "We are in the best time of our life. We have been married fifty-eight years. We are both retired, and our house is almost paid off. We have a son and daughter, four grandchildren, three greats, and one on the way. One of our granddaughter's is getting married soon. I hope he'll be well by then because she is already planning a dance with him at her wedding."

We drove a while in silence. Then he said. "I have seen this before. You might need to contact your family members. They will probably want to be with you and your husband." I didn't respond. I just tried to sort out what he might be telling me.

It was quiet again. *If this is a heart attack, I'm sure the kids would want to be here with Dad,* I thought. I didn't want to analyze what his comments might mean.

Arriving at the hospital I checked in at the front desk to let the receptionist know I was there. She told me to have a seat, and she would let me know when I could go in to see him. The fireman, Dave, stayed with me. It was very comforting to have someone by my side during my state of confusion.

My cell phone rang, it was Mindy. "Mom, did Dad die?" she asked breathless.

"No, honey. I'm at the hospital, and Dad is here. A fireman brought me, and I'm waiting for them to let me see him."

"What happened?"

"I thought he had gone inside to watch NASCAR on television. Just a few minutes later, I went inside and found him sitting in the recliner, just starring. He looked like he did when he got stung by all those horse flies a few summers ago." I didn't want to worry her.

"Darren and I are on our way, and Cory too. Is the fireman still there?"

"Yes."

"Let me talk to him."

"Okay." I handed him my cell phone Dave. "My daughter wants to speak with you."

He took the phone. "Hello."

"Hi, my name is Mindy. I'm her daughter. I want you to promise me something."

"What is it?" asked Dave.

"Will you be taking my mother back to the mobile home?"

"Yes, I suppose so."

"Please don't leave my mother alone until she is with someone she knows when you take her back."

"I won't. I'll take good care of her."

"Thank you so much for being there for us."

"No problem, good-bye." He handed the phone back to me.

"He sounds like a nice man," Mindy said. "We are on our way."

"That's good. I'll call you after I get to see Dad. Love you, and drive safe."

"Love you, Mom." I could hear her start to cry.

"See you soon." I took a deep breath and sat down.

"I'm going to go and check to see how your husband is doing, and when you can see him," said Dave.

"Thanks," I said as I watched him disappear through the large double doors. Again, another long wait. Probably not as long as it seemed. I stood up when I saw Dave walking toward me, as I tried to read the expression on his face.

"Good news," he said. "They got a heartbeat. That's a real good sign."

I let out a big sigh. I didn't realize I had been holding my breath. "Can I go see him now?"

"Just a few more minutes. They are getting ready to transfer him to the hospital at Lake Havasu."

"That's good." *They will probably have to do a bi-pass. It's a bigger hospital with better surgeons.* I felt good about this news.

A nurse came out and motioned for me to follow her. She took me into a room where he was lying on a gurney. He was connected to several machines. I guess they were to help him breathe. He didn't seem conscious, and his eyes were shut.

One of the doctors told me that a helicopter was on its way to transport Randall to Lake Havasu.

"Can I go with him?" I asked.

"I'm sorry. The helicopter is too small, and we will have a few staff on board with him."

"Okay, thank you," I said, nodding. I looked at Randall lying there, not moving. *He is probably sedated,* I thought. *At least he doesn't seem to be in any pain. That's good.*

The doctor said, "We are about ready to prepare him for the transfer."

"Can I go closer and talk to him?" There were so many machines on him that I felt like I had to ask permission.

"Yes, go right ahead. But don't touch any of the equipment."

I stood next to my husband. I wondered if he was cold because he had nothing on but his undershorts. *Maybe that's because of all the machines.* I looked at the doctor and asked, "Isn't he cold?"

"No," he replied. "But we will wrap him in blankets before we put him on the helicopter."

Will you really? I wondered. *Or are you just telling me that to make me feel better?*

I leaned over his face, in case he opened his eyes he could see me. "Honey, I'm here." *No eye twitching, nothing.* "Everything is going to be okay." *Will it?* "Can you hear me? They are going to take you in a helicopter to the hospital at Lake Havasu." *I wish I could just give him a kiss, but too many machines. I can't even hold his hand.* "Cory and Mindy are on their way." I put my hand on his arm. *He is warm.* "We'll see you when you get there. I love you. You are going to be okay." *I wonder if I could at least kiss his forehead? Maybe not. So many machines.* "I have to go now. See you soon. I love you, Randall."

€

This is harder to write than I thought. I had to stop for a minute. My hands are shaking. Reliving this is making me cry. I'm not sure I can do this.

THREE

I stepped aside as nurses prepared Randall for the transfer to Lake Havasu. As I sat and watched, I couldn't help but remember the off-the-wall things he did. As my grandmother would say, he was full of the dickens.

In the 90s, we owned a travel agency. We loved to travel and we needed something for a tax write-off. Both of us had what we called real jobs, and had two wonderful ladies that worked the store during the day.

After work, I would go to do the bookkeeping, and Randall would deliver tickets. A personal touch that really improved our business.

As owners, periodically we would receive free trips called FAM Trips. This was to familiarize the agents with resort properties. Randall always had a buildup of vacation days from his real job, and took advantage of the free travel. A few times he flew to Hawaii just for a few days.

Most of the travel agents were women, and it was nice to have a man along. Mr. Sociable, was more than willing to go. One time he went to Kona for the weekend with fourteen women. I guess you could call that perks.

***

One trip we took was to Nashville. On the plane, I would read and he would nap.

"What are you reading?" he asked me as we took off.

"Nothing Lasts Forever" by Sidney Sheldon."

"That sounds a little depressing."

"Believe me, his books are far from depressing. He's one of my favorite authors."

"What did you say his name was?"

Holding the book up for him to see. "Sidney Sheldon," I repeated.

The first day in Nashville, we walked around the town. We had tickets for the Grand Ole Opry the following night.

"I noticed a Comedy Club next to the Opry," said Randall. "How about an early dinner and then check out the club?"

"Sounds good to me."

After dinner we went to the box office and bought our tickets, which seemed very reasonable. Before seating us the usher said, "There is a ten-dollar cover change per person."

"What?" said Randall.

I knew that was going to upset him. At home he refused to go anyplace where there was a cover charge and would ask to speak with the manager. He would tell him, "My bar tab will more than compensate you for the cover charge." Then they would let us in free. I found this a little embarrassing, but it always worked, so I kept quiet.

So when the usher said there was a cover charge, Randall surprised me with his response.

"Maybe you don't know who I am? I'm the famous author, Sidney Sheldon."

What did he just say? It was difficult for me to keep a straight face.

"Well Mr. Sheldon, we are glad that you have chosen our club for your nightly entertainment. Let me seat you."

He took us to the second row, which was a lot better than the tickets we purchased. Once we were seated and thanked the usher, I whispered, "I can't believe you did that."

"It got us in, didn't it?" he said with a smile.

"But Sidney Sheldon is about twenty years older than you."

"Evidently the usher didn't know that."

The curtain opened, and a young man did his standup routine. When he was through the Master of Ceremonies took the microphone.

"Ladies and Gentleman, we are honored to have in our audience tonight the well-known author, Sidney Sheldon." He held out his hand as a motion for Mr. Sheldon to stand up.

Oh my God, what are we going to do now? I wondered. *Oh no, he's getting up, and waving to the audience. Then he quickly sat down.*

I wanted to crawl under the seats, but I guess no one really knew who Sidney Sheldon was until…

"Mr. Sheldon, may we speak to you for a minute?" said an usher, flashing his small light for Randall to follow him. I followed behind because I had a feeling we would be leaving soon.

In the lobby, two men asked him for his identification.

"Okay, guys, you caught me," said Randall. "Come on Tami, I think we are leaving." And we did.

"I can't believe you did that," I said. "I'm so embarrassed. That's the second time you've gotten me thrown out of somewhere."

He laughed aloud.

"I'm sorry, but I don't think it's funny!"

"Oh come on, honey. Don't be mad at me."

Well, I was, for at least twenty minutes, and then I was laughing with him, as we talked about him standing up and waving at the audience.

***

"Mrs. Miller, Mrs. Miller," said Dave, bringing me out of my thoughts. "If you are ready to go, I'll take you home."

"Yes, I'm ready."

"Here are your husband's things," he said, handing me a plastic bag with Randall's wallet, car keys, and glasses.

I took them thinking; *Won't he need these when he gets to the hospital? Maybe they are giving them to me for safekeeping.*

"Would you like to watch the take off?" asked Dave as we got into his truck.

"Sure." I gave Mindy a call to let her know Dad was going to be transferred to the Lake Havasu Hospital.

Dave drove to the heliport and parked. My cell phone rang, it was my daughter.

"Mom, we are on our way. Pep and Heather are waiting for you at the trailer. They will take you to Lake Havasu. We are going straight to the hospital," said Mindy. I was glad to know that our friends from Chino Hills, who have a mobile home in our park, would be able to take me to the Lake Havasu.

"That sounds perfect. I'm parked at the hospital with Dave. We are watching Dad take off in the helicopter, and I've got good news, they got a heartbeat. That's a real good sign. I'll see you soon. Drive safe. Love you."

"Love you, Mom. I know everything will be all right. See you soon."

Watching the stretcher being loaded on the helicopter was surreal. *He's going to be okay,* I told myself.

We watched the helicopter take off until it was out of sight. Dave pulled out of the hospital parking lot, and we headed home.

"I can't thank you enough for being with me during the worse day of my life. I don't know what I would have done without you." I fought back the tears. *Is this really happening?*

"I'm glad I was available to help out." Before he left, he gave me his phone number in case I needed his help again. Pep and Heather were waiting to greet us when we drove up. I thanked Dave again and he left.

Heather was holding Kissy, who wiggled out of her arms when she saw me. I took her and squeezed her tightly as I received a lot of kisses on my neck. She had to be so confused.

"I'm so glad you are here," I told Heather as we hugged, and both fought back our tears.

"How are you doing?" asked Heather.

"I really don't know. I'm glad they are taking him to Lake Havasu. I'm sure he'll get the care he needs there. Let me take Kissy to go potty and leave her some food, and then I'll be ready to go. Are you ready to take me?"

"Yes. Mindy called us, what good timing. While you take care of Kissy, we'll unload the car. We just got here. Come down when you are ready."

"Okay. Thank you, thank you," I said with another hug. I took Kissy for a short walk. When I fed her, she wouldn't eat. She just looked at me as if she knew I was going to leave her again. At home before I would go out, I would give her a treat and she wouldn't eat it. But the minute I returned she ran to gobble it up. I picked her up and held her tight.

"It's going to be okay. Dad will come home with us soon. I know you don't know what is going on. I'm not sure I do either. I'm going to be gone for a few hours. I need to check on Dad. You need to be a good girl while I'm gone." Yes, I talk to her like she's a real person, because, to me, she is. I kissed the top of her head and put her down.

I went to get my purse. Of course that was always a sign I was leaving. I turned on a few lights for her and made sure she had plenty of water, because actually, I didn't know when I would be back. Locking the door, again she started scratching at the glass. Usually I yelled at her to stop, but this time I didn't.

As I was leaving the park with Pep and Heather, I told them everything that had happened. Then I sat back for a minute, took a deep breath and again began reflecting on some of the crazy things Randall had done.

Thinking of the first time he got me thrown out of a place, I started to tell the story to Pep and Heather. "You guys know how crazy Randall can be sometimes. Especially you Pep, because you've been out drinking with him. One time we had been out partying with a few friends. One was Ray Collins, who was one of the singers with Frank Zappa group, "Mothers of Invention". In fact, Ray sang at our wedding.

"The bars were closing, and no one was ready to go home. Ray asked us to go with him to an afterhour's place where he got together with other singers late at night. He called it 'jamming'. So we went with him.

"Ray said that you have to be a singer to get in. He told Randall and Joe, another guy that came along with us. Don't worry, I'll tell the doorman you guys are with me. At the time we didn't realize that meant that Randall and Joe would have to go on stage and sing with Ray. Sure enough, when we got there, Ray told the doorman we were with him, and the group's name was, "The Hollywood Argyles," which was a current known group. The doorman hesitated but then let us all in.

"We were shown to a table where they were serving breakfast. After the waitress took our orders, Ray told Randall, 'When they call our name, just follow my lead.'

"Our food was brought to us and we had just started eating when the Master of Ceremonies announced the next act was "The Hollywood Argyles." Ray signaled to Randall and Joe to follow him to the stage.

"I grabbed Randall's arm, 'You don't know how to sing!'

"Don't worry. I'll just follow Ray."

All I could think was, *This is not good.*

"When they got on stage, Ray took out a small harmonica and blew a few notes as if to get the group in the right key. Ray started to sing, snapping his fingers in time with the music. Randall and Joe followed by snapping their fingers, and rocking back and forth.

"Randall and Joe's part was to sing, Do-Do-Whap! Do-Do-Whap! After a few, Do-Do-Whaps! We were all thrown out. I covered my face as I walked to the car, as if someone I knew might see me.

"Randall! I've never been thrown out of a place before. This is so embarrassing." Yes, I was mad at him for about twenty minutes, and then it turned into laughter about how funny he and Joe looked singing, Do-Do-Whap!"

Pep and Heather laughed. "Yes he's one of a kind," said Pep.

***

We arrived at the hospital. Pep parked in the emergency lot and the three of us went in.

€

This was an easier chapter to write. Today is Randall's birthday, January 20, 2018. He would have been seventy-nine. The family will be having dinner together tonight at La Paloma, in La Verne, one of his favorite hangouts. He probably got thrown out of there too, but I wasn't with him if he had. He never ceased to surprise me. Despite the embarrassing moments, that is one of the things I loved about him. Just harmless fun. How lucky I was to have those times with him.

FOUR

Entering the hospital at Lake Havasu, I approached the man at the reception area. "My husband has just been flown here from the Parker Hospital. Can you tell me where they have taken him? His name is Jack Randall Miller." My voice, stomach and hands were shaking.

The young man typed something on the computer and then said, "Yes, he has been admitted. Do you have his insurance card and some sort of identification?"

I took out the plastic bag with his things still in it and removed Randall's insurance and Drivers License from his wallet. I handed it to the young man and waited. He was so disinterested and slow that Heather finally said, "Did you locate his room? Her husband is in serious condition and she's anxious to get to him."

We waited, and he finally told us what floor Randall was on. "Check in at the nurses' station, and they will direct you," he said as he handed me back Randall's cards.

At the nurses' station we were told to go to the waiting room, and the doctor would come and talk to us soon. I called both Mindy and Cory to tell them that I was at the hospital, and what floor Dad was located on, and that I was waiting to see the doctor.

***

WHAT THE HELL JUST HAPPENED?

There were two couples who lived in La Verne that we were friends with, the Kings and the Brownsbergers. At one time they both had trailers in the same mobile home park as ours. Both couples moved to Lake Havasu when they retired. While we were in the waiting room Shelly, who was the daughter of the King's, appeared at the door. I yelled when I saw her and ran to give her a hug. We both cried, and then she told me she was a nurse at the hospital and heard that Randall had arrived via helicopter.

It was good to see someone I knew, and I was relieved to know that she could help keep an eye on things. "The doctor is with Randall now, and he will be in to talk to you soon," said Shelly.

I didn't ask her any questions because I didn't know what to ask, and I was sure she couldn't divulge her opinion. She left and said she would check back with me later.

Twenty minutes passed, and then the doctor entered the room. He introduced himself. We shook hands, and I introduced Pep and Heather to him.

"Well, Mrs. Miller, your husband is in serious condition, but is resting. We have him on machines to assist in his breathing." He paused.

What does that mean?

"I can fix a heart," said the doctor.

Wow! That's a relief.

"But I can't fix a brain."

A brain? What is he talking about?

"I'm afraid your husband was without oxygen too long," he continued. "All it takes is four minutes to cause brain damage."

Brain damage? Was it while I was still cleaning the patio furniture? Did it take me too long to get him on the floor? Was it my fault?

"We are going to monitor him and see if there is any change," said the doctor.

"Can I see him now?"

"Yes, the nurse will take you to his room. I'll be checking in with you later," he said and left. The three of us followed the nurse.

It was not a total shock when we entered his room, but it was more than I expected. He was on life support machines, and there were about ten different bags, hanging from a hook, hydrating and medicating him.

Going to his side, I said, "I'm here honey." His eyes were closed. I brushed his hair back. I kissed him on the forehead and continued caressing his head. That was about the only part of his face that wasn't covered by the breathing equipment. "Pep and Heather are here, too. They brought me. Mindy and Cory are on their way."

There was no indication that he heard me or that he knew I was there. I wanted to throw myself across his body and sob. I remembered when my Dad was dying of cancer, Mother and I talked to him in case he could hear us, and I was going to do the same now.

His body was warm. I took his opened hand, covering my face with it and kissed his palm. The nurse came in to check on the machines and to make sure the liquids from the bags was flowing properly.

Heather stood on the other side of the bed while Pep stood at the foot rubbing Randall's feet. Such a tender thing to do.

"Hey! What's going on?" asked Kent Brownsberger, as he walked into the room.

"Kent, what a surprise," I said as we hugged. "It's nice to see you."

"I saw Shelly in the hall, and I couldn't believe it when she told me Randall was here," he said.

Kent's wife, Caren, had been battling cancer. I wondered if he was here visiting her when he said, "Caren is on the next floor."

"How is she doing?" I asked.

"Not good," he responded.

"I'm sorry to hear that. She has been so strong throughout her cancer process. Let her know I wish her well. I'll drop by and see her."

"No, she doesn't want anyone to see her like she is now."

I introduced Pep and Heather to Kent and explained who they were and that they had brought me to the hospital. Kent stood next to Pep and started rubbing Randall's other foot. It was strange to watch, but what a loving sight.

"It's hard to see him like this," said Kent. "You know he was our leader."

"I'm sure he's glad to hear that. But, I'm afraid to ask, leader in what?" That made everyone laugh. I heard a commotion outside the room. It was Mindy, her husband Darren, and our two grown granddaughters, Tonya and Darriana.

Mindy came through the door first, rushing to hug me and looking over her shoulder at her father. "Daddy, I'm here," she said. I moved aside so she could get close to him. She took his hand. "I love you Daddy. I know you are going to be okay." She looked at me with that question in her eyes.

Tonya took one look at him, and it was too much for her. She turned and left the room with Darriana right behind her. Darren was still outside the room.

"Here, honey, you sit next to Dad, we'll talk later," I said to Mindy, and left to check on my granddaughters.

After taking a seat next to the bed and still holding his hand, Mindy looked up at Pep and Heather. "I'm so glad you were there when I called. Thank you for bringing Mom," she said. "Kent how did you know?"

"Caren is on the next floor, and I was visiting her," he responded. "Shelly came to tell me when they brought Randall in. I couldn't believe it."

"How is she doing?" asked Mindy.

"She's hanging in there," he said.

Darren stepped in the room for a minute. Pep and Kent stepped out with Heather, and Darren followed. They brought him up-to-date on what had happened.

Hugging Tonya and Darriana, I knew this was a traumatic experience for both of them. "I know it's hard to see Papa like this, when he is usually so full of life. We are all in a state of shock," I told the girls. "I know it's a lot to take in." All three of us clung on to each other. After a few minutes, I asked, "Are you ready to go back in?" I asked. They both nodded, and we went back in the room.

Mindy was still holding his hand, and I'm sure she didn't want to let go. But she got up to make room for her girls. Tonya went to one side and Darriana on the other. They both reached out and placed a hand on his arm.

"Do you think he can hear us?" asked Tonya, brushing away her tears.

"I hope so," I said. "Let's continue as if he does."

"Did you see Shelley?" Mindy asked me.

"Yes, she was the first person I saw when we were waiting to talk to the doctor."

"What did he say?"

"I'll tell you later." I didn't want to talk in front of Randall in case he could hear me.

The nurses were very patient with all the visitors. We tried to move family members in and out of the room, but none of us wanted to go out. A nurse stepped in and asked us to leave as they needed to attend to Randall. I suggested we go to the waiting room. I figured it would give me a chance to explain to everyone what the doctor had said.

"Hey," said Cory, poking his head around the door of the waiting room. I went to him and he hugged me tight, as I cried. "Oh, Mom, it's going to be okay."

Mindy rushed to him, and he held her tightly. "What has the doctor said?" he asked.

I faced all of them in the waiting room and relayed what the doctor had said about the downtime of oxygen and his comments about brain damage. The nurse came to let us know we could go back in.

Taking Cory's hand, Mindy led him into Randall's room. Together they stood by the bed holding hands. I could see they were both having a hard time seeing his father in this type of condition. None of us have ever seen him in a hospital bed unable to speak or move on his own. Previously he had had a few minor surgeries, but always was coherent, nothing like this.

"Dad," Cory said, his voice shaking. "I'm here." He reached down and took his father's motionless hand in his.

Cory's girlfriend was with him, but hung back from coming in the room. I stepped out and found her leaning against one of the walls crying. "This is really hard to see," she said.

"Grandma!" I turned and saw that our grandson Dejay had just arrived. He hugged me tightly, and Mindy joined us in the hallway.

"I'm glad you're here," she told him. "Sorry we couldn't wait for you to get off work to drive with us."

"That's okay. But a lot of things were going through my head on the long drive here," said Dejay. "Can I go in and see him?"

"Sure honey," I said. "Go on in. Cory is with him now."

Standing outside the room we all talked about how unbelievable this was. Randall was such a lively man, not only physically but mentally too.

Dejay came out of the room, visibly shaken. "Papa had so many good stories to tell," he said. "I'm sure we haven't heard them all yet."

Darren spoke up. "It was just a few weeks ago that I was having a beer with him at La Paloma. One of his friends told me about the time Randall offered to give him a ride home. He stopped at a store and bought a six pack. 'Let's have a beer before I take you home,' said Randall. His friend agreed that was a good idea. Randall pulled in the driveway and the two went into the backyard. They popped open a beer as they sat on the patio furniture. His friend commented, 'This is really a nice home you have here.' 'I don't live here,' said Randall. 'You don't. Who does?' asked his friend. Randall replied, 'I don't know. We probably should leave.' His friend jumped up and ran to the car and ready to leave by the time he got there. 'I can't believe you did that,' said his friend. 'Me neither,' said Randall as they drove away laughing.

"Papa is a crazy man," said Dejay. "I want to be just like him."

Pep and Heather said they were going back to the trailer. I handed Heather my house key, and asked, "Would you check on Kissy for me?"

"Sure," said Heather. I hugged both of them, and thanked them again. Mindy walked them out and soon returned.

Cory came out from the room and took Mindy's hand pulling her out-of-sight. I assumed he needed to talk to her without me hearing. When they returned, Mindy said, "Look who I found wandering the halls."

With her was Randall's sister, Judy, from Phoenix, followed his cousin Debbie with her daughter Jessica, both from Temecula. They both arrived in the lobby at the same time. I embraced all three of them. "I'm so glad you are all here with us," I said. "You girls can go in and see him. I'm not sure he hears us, but let him know you are here, and talk to him as if he can hear."

The rest of us waited outside his room, taking turns going in and out. The head nurse came to tell me, "The doctor will be back in an hour or so to talk with you and explain what is going on."

"That's good," I said. "We are lost on what to expect." I could see through the windows that it was getting dark outside. I turned to Mindy, Cory, and the rest of the group. "You guys are probably hungry. I'm sure there is a cafeteria here. Why don't you go get something to eat?"

"Are you hungry, Mom?" asked Mindy.

"No, my stomach is in knots. But I could use a cup of coffee."

"We'll bring you back a cup and maybe some soup," said Mindy. "You need to eat. It might be a long night."

"You guys go now. We will meet with the doctor when you get back." They left and I returned to sit next to Randall. It was quiet, and I was glad to be alone with him. So many questions were whirling around in my head. *I wonder what our future is? Our life is in such a good place.* I took his hand in mine. *He looks so peaceful. Does he know what is going on? I'm so scared.*

€

I was amazed how the family rallied around in such a short time. I felt blessed to have such a loving family and friends. I couldn't believe the timing that Pep and Heather arrived at the park when I needed them the most. I will never forget their friendship. Our friends' daughter Shelly being on duty, and Caren Brownsberger being in the same hospital, and her husband Kent coming by to see Randall. I was wonderful having support coming from all directions.

FIVE

Looking at Randall, I wondered what the doctor was going to tell me.

"Mom," said Mindy, entering the room. "Here's your coffee, and I brought you some soup."

"I probably need to eat something. I'll give it a try."

"Everyone is returning to the waiting room," said Mindy. "We've discussed that we are too many to be in the room at the same time and are trying to take turns."

The nurse entered and said, "The doctor will be here in twenty-minutes."

"Thanks," I replied. "I'm sorry there are so many of us."

"I know you are all concerned. We only have one other patient on this floor now, so just try to keep it quiet." Then she left.

"I'll go tell the others," said Mindy. "Do you think he'll talk with us in here?"

"I don't know. Why don't you ask the nurse if everyone can be in here with us?"

"All right. If she says okay. I'll go tell the rest."

She left, and I waited. The nurse came in and checked on all Randall's equipment.

"He's hot," she said, and removed the sheet that had covered him. He had nothing on but a diaper. This really bothered me because I knew he would never want to be seen like this.

Mindy and Cory were the first to walk in the room. I saw the shocked look on their faces when they saw their dad uncovered.

"I know what you are thinking, but he is hot," I told them.

"Mom, take a closer look at Dad," said Mindy. "His body looks so healthy, and he even looks younger."

I looked, and yes there was a transformation that was unexplainable. He actually did look younger. I had read in the Bible that when you go to Heaven, you become your best self. *Has his soul already gone?* I wondered.

Mindy left the room to warn the grandkids not to be alarmed when they saw Dad. When they came in, they all agreed how good he looked. It was unexplainable.

When Judy came in, she told us that she had called their brother, Bob, who lived in Oregon. He was the oldest. "He's not taking this very well," said Judy. "He is so broken up he couldn't talk any longer. He said he wished he could be here with all of us."

The doctor entered the room and went straight to Randall to check the equipment and all the labels on the bags.

"Is everyone here that needs to be?" he asked.

"Let me get the rest of them," said Mindy. She left the room, and they all returned following behind her.

"Well, you have quite a family," said the doctor with a smile, as he looked around the room. "I wish I had some good news to tell you."

I thought I was ready for what the doctor had to say, but I wasn't. Thinking the worse is one thing, but hearing it said aloud was like a hard blow to the heart and body.

He continued. "I have not found any indication that he is responsive. But to be sure, I suggest we leave him on life support through the night. I will check back with you in the morning."

"What exactly happened?" I asked, crying. "Was it a heart attack?" Mindy and Cory were hanging on both sides of me as if they were afraid I was going to collapse.

"No," said the doctor. "It was a blood clot that went to the heart and then to the brain. It happened very fast. I doubt if he even knew when it happened. He was never in any pain. He was probably already gone when you found him in his chair." He paused as we all tried to grasp what he was telling us. "Any questions?"

"What is the possibility that he could come out of this?" asked Cory.

"There is no kind way to put it, but I don't see any possibility of a recovery," he responded. He looked around for any additional questions; there were none. "I'll see you in the morning." Then he left.

No one in the room moved. We just looked at each other. Slowly, half of the family left. I heard someone outside the room, and one of the voices was my great-granddaughter, Laney. I stepped outside to see who else was there. It was Tonya's husband, Ryan and their two children, Laney, who was five years old, and Liam, who was three. Tonya ran to Ryan to be consoled as she sobbed in his arms. Laney came running to me for a big hug.

I watch as Tonya tried to control her tears and hugged both her children. "Do you think I can take Laney into see Papa?" she asked me.

"I don't know, she is so young," I responded. "Do you think all the machines will scare her?"

"She wants to see her Papa," said Tonya.

We had taken care of Laney since she was three-months-old, so Tonya could go back to work. There was a special bond between Laney and her Papa.

"I'll go in first," I told Tonya, "so she will know it's okay." I stood by Randall's bedside as Tonya brought in Laney. She hung back, close to her mother.

"Do you want to come closer?" I asked Laney. "It's okay."

"Do you want to tell Papa you love him?" asked Tonya. "He can hear you."

WHAT THE HELL JUST HAPPENED?

Slowly Laney walked around to his bedside, standing next to me. "Honey, Laney is here," I said to Randall. "Do you want to take his hand?" I asked Laney.

She did, and quietly said, "I love you Papa. Is he asleep?"

"Yes, but it's a special sleep. He can hear you, and I know he loves you too." She let go of his hand, returned to her mother. Tonya took her out of the room. I was glad because I was at a breaking point, watching her scared little face. *What must she be thinking?* I wondered.

I could see through the windows that it was dark outside. I had no idea what time it was. The day had been long but it seemed to have gone so fast. Mindy brought me another cup of coffee.

"We're not going back to the trailer," she said. "It's too far in case there is a change and we need to rush back. There's a motel nearby and we are all going to get a room there. Do you want to go with us?"

"No. I'm going to stay here. I just can't leave him." I couldn't hold back my tears any longer.

"Mom, do you want me to stay with you?"

"No, you guys need your sleep. No telling what is in store for us tomorrow," I said, drying my eyes with my hand.

"Tonya, Darriana, and I are going to find a drug store and buy some toiletries and then we'll be back."

"Okay honey. Would you get me a toothbrush?"

"Sure. We'll be right back." We hugged, and they left.

Cory came in and sat on the opposite side of the bed from me, just staring at his dad. A few times I saw his lips quiver. It must be hard being a man, feeling like you have to hold in all your emotions.

He looked at me, and said. "You know he never missed any of my games or practices. The coach used to ask me, 'How does he find us?' because sometimes the practices were not at the school, but he would always be there."

"He was so proud of you," I said. "I'm sure he never told you, but he was very proud."

"I know, Mom, but he had a way of causing a commotion. I remember I was catching at one of the Senior League games, and Dad did not like the umpires call. He started yelling at him and the coach had to calm him down. 'Who is that idiot?' the umpire asked me. I didn't look at him, I just said, 'That's my dad.'

"Another time I was pitching, and Dad didn't like the call and came running out on the field. That time he got escorted off the field by security. Both times I was so embarrassed. Now I look back and can only laugh at it."

"I know. When you played football I ended up sitting in the stands by myself. Your dad was on the field walking the sidelines with the coaches. It's a wonder he didn't get kicked out."

"The coaches loved Dad. Except when he caused problems."

"Well, one thing, the three times you got a concussion, your dad was the first one on the field."

"I know. He was always there."

Mindy and Tonya came back loaded down with shopping bags. They had gone to CVS and Mindy bought blankets for all the women. They are now called 'Papa blankets'.

Tonya bought me a nice sweatshirt. "I saw you shaking, Grandma," she said. "I could tell you were cold."

"Thanks honey. I love it, but I wasn't cold, it was just my nerves. I'll wear the sweatshirt tonight."

It was around nine o'clock, and we were all exhausted. Slowly, one by one, everyone came in and told Randall goodnight, and gave me a hug before leaving.

A few minutes later, they were all gone and it was just the two of us. He still lay uncovered. Several times I stood up and kissed his head and said, "Please don't leave me." I looked for an answer or an eyelid to flicker, and then I sat back down. I moved my chair as close to his bed as I could get it. I lay my hand on his chest as he breathed, and then I ran my fingers through the hair on his chest. I loved doing that when we were in bed together. I loved it when he put his arm around me at night. *Will I ever have that again?* I wondered.

The nurse brought in a recliner for me to sleep on. I put on my new sweatshirt and covered up with my Papa blanket, but sleep did not come. Listening to his life support machines keeping him alive, I found myself breathing with him.

Several times during the night I went to his bedside. "Honey I'm here." I kissed his forehead, and then went back to the recliner. *How long will they let these machines keep him alive? Am I the one who has to decide?*

€

I still haven't removed his voice from my answering machine. When the kids call, they say, "Hi Papa, tell Grandma I called." When Mindy or Cory call, they say, "Hi Dad, tell Mom I called."

Both Laney, and my other great-granddaughter Kennedi, who just turned eight, go to the cemetery with me to take flowers and clean off his headstone. One time on the way home, Laney said to me, "Grandma, I forgot what Papa sounds like."

I dialed my home number on my cell phone. "Here, honey," I said handing her my phone for her to hear her Papa voice say, "Sorry we're not home. Leave a message."

She handed me back the phone. "Yeah Grandma, that's Papa."

SIX

I must have dozed off. I was afraid to open my eyes. I hoped it was all just a bad dream. But, the sound of the machines keeping Randall alive soon convinced me it wasn't. *Is this the end of our journey together?* I wondered. *What made him pick me to spend the rest of his life with?*

He was engaged when we met, and I was going steady with someone else for almost a year. It must have been what they call chemistry. I knew he was a bit of a bad boy when we married, all the warning signs were there. At eighteen, I buckled up, and he took me on one hell of a roller coaster ride.

"Mom," said Mindy as she entered the room. "Are you awake?"

"Yes. Just sitting here with my eyes closed thinking about my life with your dad. What time is it?"

"It's six-thirty in the morning. I couldn't sleep. In fact, most of us are in the waiting room. Has there been any change?"

"No, he's just the same."

"Can you come and talk with us?"

"Sure. Let me brush my teeth and do something with my hair," I said, as I ran my fingers over my head.

"I'll get you some coffee and meet you in the waiting room." Before she left, she stopped at her dad's bedside. "Good morning, Daddy. It doesn't look like you will be pruning any trees today." She took his hand and pressed it against her cheek. "Don't you worry about it. I'll take care of it from now on." She kissed his hand and laid it back on the bed. Tears were streaming down her face as she left.

Before I joined the family, I went to Randall's side. "Good morning, honey." I brushed back his hair and kissed his forehead. "Can you hear me? I love you." Then I left to meet with the family.

Everyone was there except Ryan who had taken the kids to the trailer to spend the night.

"Mom," said Mindy. "We all talked about Dad's situation last night."

"And?"

"We think you might have to make some decisions today," said Mindy. She paused, and I waited to hear what she had to say.

Cory spoke up. "If we can't have Dad back as Dad, and if he can't go out every morning and work in the yard, we need to let him go."

I looked at everyone's faces. Slowly, they all nodded in agreement, including Tonya, who was sobbing. By the looks of her blood shot eyes, she must have cried all night.

"I'm glad you all feel that way," I said. "Because you are right. It would not be fair for him to spend the rest of his life in a wheelchair or to be bedridden. He would never forgive us. We'll see what the doctor has to say this morning, but I don't see any change."

"Grandma," said Tonya. "How did Papa ask you to marry him?"

"Well, honey, let me tell you." I took a seat between Tonya and Darriana.

"Your Papa and I had been dating for about seven months. He broke off his engagement with his girlfriend, and I broke up with the guy I had been dating when I met your Papa. Back then it was called going steady, not sure what they call it today.

"It's no secret that Papa liked his beer and sometimes a cocktail or two. We had met several of our friends for a beach party at Thousand Steps in Laguna. Needless-to-say there was a lot of drinking going on. When all the beer was gone, Dad's friend Gary asked us to go with him and his girlfriend, Sherry, to Balboa where his parents had a beach house. He said they had a liquor cabinet, and it was probably full.

"When we got there, Dad and Gary were a little disappointed that the cupboard was empty. Dad said he heard that there was a party a few streets over where some of his friends were. I was partied out and so was Sherry, so we didn't go. He left with Gary and said they were going to check it out and would be right back.

"Gary came back in about twenty minutes. He said they went to another party and got separated, and he didn't know what happened to Randall. Then he left with Sherry, and there I sat; not very happy. Dad had left his car keys in my purse. I taught dancing lessons at Co-Op Dance Studio in Pomona and had classes early in the morning. So I took his car and left. I thought I would teach him a lesson.

"When he came back to Gary's parents' house, we were all gone, he thought I had left with Gary, and someone had stolen his car. He went back to one of the parties and found a friend who lived in La Verne and asked him for a ride home.

"The next morning he had his Dad give him a ride to Pomona to my dance studio, which was on the second floor over the Larry Welling Jewelry Store. There was an alley next to it and below the dance studio. As I was teaching, I was counting out dance steps for my class. One-two-three-four. But when I got to four, a loud voice from the alley, yelled 'four'. After the second 'four', I went to the window overlooking the alley. It was your Papa. He yelled he was sorry and asked if I had his car. He wanted to take me to lunch. I told him, yes, I had his car, but no, I wouldn't go to lunch with him. He said he would keep yelling from the alley if I didn't go. By this time the five, seven-year-old little girls were hanging their heads out the window too.

One of the little girls in the class asked, "Is that your boyfriend?"

"Yes, he is," I responded. "Okay, I'll go to lunch with you, but you need to leave," I shouted down to the alley. He waved and disappeared in the back parking lot - probably looking for his car.

"I met him downstairs for lunch, and we drove to Lincoln Park. He said he was so sorry about last night, and it would never happen again. Then he got down on one knee, just like in the movies, and pulled out a black velvet box. When he opened it, it was the biggest diamond ring I had ever seen. He asked me to marry him, and of course I said yes. That was fifty-eight years ago."

"Wow, Grandma" said Tonya. "That's a funny story."

"Yes, he's a funny guy," I agreed.

The nurse entered our room. "The doctor is with Randall now and is ready to meet with you."

"Can we all go in?" I asked.

"Yes," she said. "He said it would be okay."

We all filed in and circled around Randall's bed. I held his hand as we listened to the doctor speak.

"Good morning, everyone," he said. "I've reviewed Mr. Miller's activity during the night, and there was no change. I know this is a hard decision to make. We can keep him on life support if you wish…"

I interrupted him, "Doctor, my husband was a very active man, and loved his independence." I took a deep breath. "If we can't bring him back to be the man he was, we are all in agreement to let him go."

When I said that, the strangest thing happened. The sound of Randall's machines stopped for a minute, and it was very quiet. We all turned and looked at him, and then the machines started again. We took that as him saying, "Thank you." As hard as it was, we knew it was the right thing to do.

"You have made the right decision," said the Doctor. "He is a lucky man to have such a loving family."

As he left, we all shook hands with him. The nurse came in and said, "When you are ready we will disconnect his life support."

Oh my God! I thought, as reality set in. I wanted to yell, NO! I've changed my mind, but I knew we were making the right decision. Knowing what I had to do next, I said, "Let's all go out, and you can each have a private moment to say good-bye." Saying that, I lost it. I started to cry, and I had a hard time breathing. Cory put his arm around me and walked me out of the room.

Mindy took control and asked who would like to go first. Her son, Dijay, spoke "I will Mom," he said. After a few minutes he came out with his eyes watering. One by one, we each went in to say good-by. We were all overwhelmed with emotions.

The nurse asked if anyone wanted to be in the room while she disconnected the life support. "I want to be with him," I said and walked in with the nurse. I took Randall's hand and said, "This is not good-bye. I love you, and we will be together again."

Trying to get my breath as I sobbed, I watched while the nurse disconnected all the IV's and turned off the breathing machine. He didn't take one breath. I wasn't ready for what happened next. Once all the liquids were drained from his body, it was unbearable to watch. His face sunk in and the flesh looked like it was drying up before my very eyes.

"I can't stand to watch this," I said, and rushed out of the room. *He's really gone!*

The worse thing was, I never got to tell him good-bye or that I loved him that one last time. I hoped that while he was lying in the hospital, he could hear us saying our goodbyes and how much he meant to us. I wondered if he knew the impact he had on each of our lives. I wanted to believe he heard all our loving words.

His journey here on earth has ended. But he will rejoice being with his mother, dad, and grandparents.

What will my life be like now without him? Honestly I never before gave it a thought. Will I be strong enough to support my family while they morn? My head is swimming. What am I suppose to do next?

€

The last words I said to him when we were at the river, "I hope you aren't going to mow the yard."

WHAT THE HELL JUST HAPPENED?

Afterward, when I talked with my friends, and they would tell me about their own experience during the passing of a loved one, following a long illness, I wanted to yell at them, "It's not the same!" But I didn't.

I asked Mindy if she could remember the last thing she said to Dad. She reminded me of coming to the house the night before we left for the river.

She had been walking after work, late at night, and Randall worried about her being out in the dark. Even when she walked in the canyon on the weekends during the day, her phone would go dead. He would panic and go find her to make sure she was okay.

So he wouldn't worry so much, she got a flashing red light and attached it to the back of her belt. She came by the house Wednesday night to show her dad. When she turned her back to show him the blinking light, she asked, "Does this make my butt look big?"

Such an important time, but how would we have known that we would never get to tell him we loved him, and he would not get to hear us say it.

SEVEN

I ran out of the room straight into my son's arms.

"I gotcha Mom," he said, as he held me and let me sob.

I took a tissue from the box on the nurse's counter and wiped away my tears. I wasn't the only one crying. We hugged each other, and then stood holding hands. I looked at the nurse and asked, "Do I need to sign anything?"

"Your son has taken care of that," she responded.

"Mom, they have called this mortuary," said Cory, and showed me their business card. "Dad will be sent there. We will need to make an appointment to meet with them."

Addressing the head nurse, I said, "I want to thank you and all your staff for being so wonderful to us." They had set up a coffee station for my family that morning with a selection of muffins and sweet rolls. I turned to my family. "If there's nothing else, I guess we can leave."

Judy, Randall's sister, hugged all of us again and said she was going to return home. Debbie and her daughter were ready to go home too. I thanked them for being with us. It was good we were all together.

The rest of us decided to go back to the trailer and talk about what to do next. Honestly, I was so tired and felt brain dead. I still wondered, *what the hell just happened.*

Tonya and her family, and Darriana came to the trailer before they headed home. Mindy also had a trailer in the same mobile home park. Her husband and son were going to leave in the morning. Mindy, Cory, and his girlfriend stayed because they were going to the mortuary with me.

It was three o'clock in the afternoon, and we were all tired. I don't remember eating anything, but I'm sure I did. I called the mortuary and made an appointment for eleven o'clock the next morning.

Around five o'clock, I went to bed. My mind was rushing and crashing as I tried to understand what my life was going to be like now. I had heard the expression 'broken hearted.' I now know what that meant. I truly felt like my heart was broken in tiny little pieces. It actually hurt.

I'm a planner and normally well organized, but I hadn't planned on this and I was too tired to think straight. I thought about my mother and the plans we made to bury my Dad. He had been sick with cancer for over a year, and I know they had discussed plans together. I had helped her with many of the arrangements. At the time, I hadn't thought that one day I would be faced with preparing to lay my husband to rest.

My mind then went to the time I buried my mother. I'm an only child, so I was responsible for making all the decisions. Mindy was helpful to me while making the arrangements. Mother had been ill for several years. She had no other living relatives, so the process was easy to handle.

As I lay in bed, I remembered picking out her casket and ordering the flowers. She already had her plot at Forest Lawn in Covina, next to my Dad. The service was held at the chapel at Forest Lawn, and I had a small reception at my home. She was eighty-seven and most of those attending the service were my family and people from my work.

Now, my life as I knew it was over. I finally fell asleep.

***

The next morning we all got together for coffee and planned the day. Darren and Dejay left for home, and we got ready for our meeting at the mortuary at Lake Havasu.

Once there, we were greeted by a woman representative. She extended her condolences and said her name was Stacy, and she would be our funeral counselor. She then took us into a conference room. I wasn't sure what to expect because I thought all the final arrangements would be done once we were home and met with Todd's Mortuary in Pomona.

Stacy handed me an application to fill out. It required a lot of information about Randall's parents, brother, and sister. I thought I knew where everyone was born, but I didn't know the county. Concerned I wasn't thinking clearly, I called Randall's sister to verify some of the information.

Reviewing the application, Stacy said, "We will have to get Mr. Miller's death certificate before we can request the permit to transport him to California."

Permit? I thought. *I guess so because Lake Havasu is in Arizona. Who would think he would need a permit to go home.*

"This is Saturday," said Stacy. "We probably won't receive his death certificate until late on Monday, and then it will take a few days to get the permit to transport him. How many copies of the death certificate do you want to order?"

"I don't know," I responded.

"I suggest you get about twelve. You will be surprised how many you will need. Many places will require an original, not a copy. If you order them now, you will save money. If you need to get more originals later, they will cost you about twenty-five dollars each."

"Okay. I'll take twelve certificates," I replied.

She then handed me another document. "We will need your authorization for embalming." Attached was a list of fees, which they called professional services. I reviewed the list: embalming, cosmetology, casketing, positioning, shipping, restoration, hairdresser, and refrigerated transportation. That was just the short list.

It was all overwhelming. I felt like I was in the brink of a meltdown. "Would you excuse us for a minute?" I said. "I need some fresh air." I didn't wait for an answer. I stood up, and Cory and Mindy followed me outside.

Leaning against the building, I tried to compose myself. "I don't know how people do this," I mumbled. "So many emotions." I paused and took a deep breath. "We can do this," I told them.

"Yes, we can," agreed Mindy

My kids were concerned about me, and I was concerned about them. "I'm so glad you are here with me," I said and started to cry. Of course, every time I cried, Mindy cried too. "I don't think I can do this without both of you." Cory, trying to console us struggled to maintain his own emotions. This was just the beginning. I stopped crying.

We returned to the conference room, and I signed the authorization to embalm. Stacy then presented us with a picture album of caskets. Neither I nor the kids were ready for this.

I thought this was something we would decide at Todd's Mortuary when we got home. "Do we have to pick this out now?" I asked.

"You don't have to," said Stacy, "but it will make it easier to transport him to California."

"What if I waited to pick out the casket at Todd's?" I remembered picking out the casket for my mother and dad. Todd's had a room to review them, and you could actually see what you were buying. I really didn't want to make this choice from a picture book.

"If you don't select one now, he will be transported in a plain wood box" said Stacy.

"A plain box?" I asked. Stacy nodded. *That wouldn't be right,* I thought. So we started to thumb though the album and settled on a nice mahogany one.

"Will you be sending me his clothes that you want him buried in?" asked Stacy. I had a quick vision of him being transported in a plain box in his underpants.

"I'll ship you his clothes as soon as I get home."

I'm sure Cory and Mindy were shocked at all the decisions that had to be made and the cost. It was a painful, but a meaningful experience for them.

Leaving the mortuary, we went to a restaurant and talked about what we had to accomplish and made a list of what we needed to do once we were home.

We were all exhausted when we returned to our mobile home. I laid down for a short nap.

That night, the four of us had dinner together, and as strange as it might seem, we actually laughed about some of the things Randall had done. One side of him was serious and strict and followed all life rules. The other side was crazy and unpredictable.

The next morning, Mindy drove me home in Randall's truck. Cory and his girlfriend went home to Laguna.

I knew there were more decisions to come, but first I had to return to my empty house. Kissy sat on my lap all the way home; periodically, she would start to shake. I would talk to her softly and hold her close, and the shaking would stop. She knew something was not right. Where was Dad?

As soon as we entered the house, Kissy ran to the bedroom looking for Randall. He wasn't there. Then she ran back to his chair in the family room. She stood on her hind legs to see if she could see him. He wasn't there. She ran to the back door and scratched to go out. When I opened the door, she ran to the middle of the yard and looked around. Then she ran to the dog run in our lower yard. Maybe he was there? But no.

That night, at bedtime, I lifted Kissy on the bed where she slept at our feet. She sat there awake, staring at the bedroom door waiting for him to come in. The next morning she dashed to the backyard again, running from one corner to the next. Where was Dad? This went on for several weeks. One night when I put her on the bed to sleep, she wanted down. Kissy no longer sleeps on the bed at night. She now sleeps under the bed on Randall's side.

***

A few years ago we attended one of Cory's friend's father's funeral. The reception was at the Mining Company, a restaurant nearby. I remembered Randall telling me, "When I die I want to have my celebration here, and I don't want anyone to pay for their drinks."

"Okay," I said. "I'll make sure that happens!" And we both laughed.

***

I called the kids to check on their availability to go to Todd's to plan the funeral service and to go to the Mining Company to discuss the plan for Randall's celebration of life."

The first problem we had at Todd's was that Randall was still in Arizona. We couldn't even pick a date for the service. The funeral director asked us how many we expected to attend. *How do you come up with that number?* I wondered. *People don't RSVP for funerals.*

"We need to know how many programs to make and how many police escorts to have," said the director. We decided about a hundred people would be there. That was just a guess. As we talked about the service schedule, I realized I hadn't made an appointment with the cemetery. Randall had told me many times he wanted to be buried in the La Verne Cemetery where his parents were laid-to-rest.

We finished working out the schedule for the service to be at the end of two weeks. Randall would certainly be here by then. I called the mortuary at Lake Havasu, and they said they would transfer him by the end of the week.

Our appointment with the Mining Company was later that afternoon. I tried to get as much done in one day because Cory and Mindy had to take the day off work.

€

With so much to do and still more decisions to make, I continued with my morning walks, because I knew it was healthy and it was my quiet time. Music was an emotional trigger, so I stopped listening to my I-Pod when I walked. Returning home was the hardest, knowing that Randall was not going to be there to say, "How was your walk?" Such a simple thing made me cry all the way home.

Randall's truck was still in the driveway. Every time I looked out the kitchen window, I thought, *He's home*. On the third day, I called my son-in-law. "Please come get Randall's truck and park it somewhere else." He did, and it was soon sold. I laid my head on the tailgate of the truck as if to hug it before it left my driveway, saying good-bye to another piece of the life we had together.

EIGHT

Cory, Mindy, and I met with the event planner at the Mining Company. They had five conference rooms upstairs, and the main dining room and bar were on the lower floor. They usually have larger parties in the conference room, but it turned out that they were closed on Mondays, which was the day of the service. They offered us the downstairs for Randall's Celebration of Life. That was great news because we knew if it was up to him, he would pick the bar area.

The next afternoon we had an appointment at the small La Verne Cemetery. I thought the only available plots would be by the back wall, or they would have to take out part of the hedge to make room for him. Meeting with the representative, I asked him to show Cory and Mindy where Randall's parents were buried.

As we stood by their gravesites, Cory asked, "Are there any plots available near here?"

The representative took out a cemetery map and was reviewing it when Cory noticed an area next to Randall's father that looked vacant. "Is this area available?" asked Cory.

I knew that many people had plots reserved in advance. Certainly that one had already been taken. As the representative studied the plot map, he looked up at us with a smile and said, "That plot is available."

We couldn't believe it. Randall could be buried next to his father. I thought, *it was meant to be. God must have saved that place for him.*

"We'll take it!" I said, and ordered a stacked interment. I was at peace to know that once again we would be together, and my children would not have to deal with that decision. We went home in disbelief and satisfied with the day's events.

It had been a good day, but returning to an empty house was a hard adjustment. Cory and Mindy went home to their loved ones. At least I had Kissy. Later that night I shared with her where Dad would be staying. I promised to take her there for a visit.

Mindy helped me write the obituary for the newspaper. Tonya and Darriana worked on putting together a video of Randall's life for his service, and Hayley made a slide presentation to be shown at the Mining Company.

At first I had been upset that we had to wait for over two weeks for the funeral. But now, I was glad I had all that time to prepare. Todd's Mortuary called to let me know that Randall had arrived. That gave me relief.

During the week, family and friends who were coming from out of state and out of town were making arrangements for overnight stays and periodically came by the house or call to check on me. Beautiful plants and flowers were being delivered to the house. I hoped Randall was looking down to see how many people loved him.

A friend of Cory and Mindy's, Craig Lawrence, was the pastor of a local church. Mindy called him and made arrangements for him to meet with us. It was nice to know the service was going to be conducted by someone who knew the family. Ivan De Herrera, one of Cory's close friends who had traveled with him and Randall on several Mexico and river trips, was going to do the eulogy. We met with both of them at the house during the week.

It was two days before the service. Tonya and Darriana had the video finished and wanted me to view it. I knew it was going to be a difficult task, but I had to do it. Mindy and the girls came over that night so we could watch it together. It was wonderful. Needless to say I was a basket case reliving all the memories and our time together. After they left and all through the night and into the next morning, I felt so lost and broken. I had a meltdown and couldn't stop crying.

***

On the day of the service, Darren's friend, Chris Leggios, made arrangements for a limo to come to our house to take the family to the funeral home. A nice jester from a good friend. I was looking forward to putting this day behind me, because I knew it was going to be extremely emotional.

When we arrived at Todd's I was surprised to see a few of our friends had already there. I greeted them and stood at the entrance. The flower arrangements were abundant. I saw the casket and the top of Randall's forehead and face from where I was standing in the foyer. My legs went weak, and Mindy helped me to the closest chair to sit down. I couldn't go any closer. I had requested a closed casket, because I knew I couldn't bear to see him like that. But, the casket was open before the service so other family members could pay their respects and have a private moment with him. I had an option for a viewing the night before, which I passed on. More people started arriving, and the funeral director closed the casket.

Cory and Mindy were still in the foyer with me and greeted people as they arrived. "Mom, they have closed the casket," said Mindy. "Do you want to go in now and sit down?" I agreed, and the family joined me in the front two rows. "Mom, you won't believe how many people are here," she said looking at those sitting behind us. "The balcony is even full."

"There aren't any more seats. People are standing outside," said Cory as he joined us.

The funeral director came to me and said, "Mrs. Miller, I need your approval to add two more traffic escorts. The gathering is a lot larger than we planned for."

"Certainly," I responded. *I don't recognize half these people,* I thought. *He touched so many lives.*

Todd's representative stood behind the podium and welcomed everyone, and then introduced Craig Lawrence. He stepped forward and told how he knew our family, and then he introduced Ivan, who told the story about taking Mindy in his car when she was fifteen for an ice cream cone. He didn't know that she wasn't allowed to go with any boys in their car. Randall was waiting in the front yard, standing on the curb, when they returned. Ivan said when he saw Randall he thought he was going to kill him as he tried to explain he had just taken her to get an ice cream cone.

He shared one of his adventures with Randall and Cory to La Paz for the Baja One Thousand. He explained that Randall had a way of causing mischief for him and others. Fortunately, or unfortunately, Ivan looked just like the movie star, Tom Selleck. Randall had attended many off-road races and knew the people who were running the event. When he introduced his son, Cory, he also introduced Ivan as Tom Seleck. Ivan, being Ivan, thought it was funny and enjoyed the attention, especially when girls started to ask him for his autograph.

That night, before the race, the mayor sponsored a dinner for the racers. As his special quests, he invited Tom Seleck, and his two friends, Randall and Cory. The three received VIP treatment throughout the race. They were now in over their heads with no way to turn back. I remember Randall telling me this story to the point when it was time to leave the airport, girls were at the outside fence with pad and pens yelling Tom's name wanting his autograph as they boarded the plan.

Everyone at the service was laughing as he told these stories. The video followed, and the tears returned to many of us.

Randall's favorite song was "Purple Rain" by Prince. Hayley's boyfriend, Stephen Wesley, a singer and songwriter, sang it while playing his acoustic guitar as everyone filed out past the casket.

WHAT THE HELL JUST HAPPENED?

Following the group, the family mingled among those attending, receiving hugs and condolences as we thanked them for joining us.

A man stopped me before I got into the limo to go to the gravesite. "Tami," he said to get my attention. "Do you remember me? I'm the one who introduced you to Randall." I didn't recognize him right away, but when he said that, I immediately knew who he was. I threw my arms around his neck, "Johnny!" I exclaimed. "How nice of you to come." I had dated Johnny before Randall, but hadn't seen him for over sixty years.

"Mom," said Mindy, "we need to go." She took my arm and guided me to the car. Yes, even funerals have a schedule. We had allotted a certain amount of time for the service and the gravesite, so we would arrive at the Mining Company at the committed time.

Randall's family moved from Oklahoma to California when he was seven. Growing up in San Dimas and La Verne, he still had many friends dating back to his grammar school years.

When the hearse arrived at the cemetery, the pallbearers removed the casket and proceeded to the gravesite followed by eight of his schoolmates, who we called Randall's crew.

I had asked our friend, Lynette Morgan's daughter, Keri Tafoya, to sing, "Amazing Grace". She had a beautiful voice; it was very moving.

When we arrived at the Mining Company, many of our guests were already there. The food was served, drinks were flowing, and toasts were being made to Randall. He would have loved it. After eating, we played the slide show that Hayley had put together; so many friends, so many memories. Then Stephen played and sang "Purple Rain" again. We all stood up and sang along, and the waterworks started all over again.

***

It's was over. Time to return to my empty house. Kissy was waiting. I sobbed, as I held her so tight. It's a wonder she didn't cry out. Now all I could think, was, **WHAT DO I DO WITH THE REST OF MY LIFE?** I wanted to go to the back yard and scream as loud as I could. But I didn't.

I tried to maintain some type of normalcy, as the days passed. I was in the midst of writing my fourth book, "Tragedy, Tears, and Trust" of my series, "Family Forever." In that book, I write about my father dying. It was really difficult writing about his death, as I was grieving over losing my husband. Because of that it took me longer to complete those chapters. I started and stopped. I cried. I started and stopped many times.

€

After the funeral I wanted to be with Randall again, now, not later. I would never do it, but I could understand why people committed suicide when times become so desperate. The loneliness and times of despair; one just wants to make the hurt stop. You only think about yourself, not the ones left behind. I've know a few people who have taken their life in their own hands. I think they don't consider, suicide is permanent, and the hurt they leave for their loved ones left behind.

NINE

Before Randall passed away I looked for ways to give back to the community by volunteering. I called several places to check out their programs. Many businesses that I contacted wanted a daily or monthly commitment. I wasn't ready to commit to daily timeframes. We were still traveling; sometimes leaving on the spur of a moment.

I saw an article in the newspaper about a club starting up in La Verne. It was new in our area but certainly not new in existence. It is called, "General Federation Of Women's Club". I called for information. It only once a month in the evening. I certainly could work around that. The local club represented two cities, La Verne, where I live, and the neighborhood city San Dimas.

The club had already had their first meeting in August, 2015. The next meeting was September. When I arrived, there were only a dozen ladies in attendance. I was surprised that I didn't know any of them considering I had lived in La Verne close to forty years. Everyone was so cordial. It is a non-profit organization that does volunteer work in the community; just what I was looking for. They were in the beginning stages of forming their charitable project list. The president, Linda Koontz, explained more projects would be added as the membership as it grew, and that I did not have to participate in all the projects. I could pick the ones that interested me. I joined on the spot. The next meeting was October, and I looked forward to attending.

Randall died two weeks before the October meeting. I called the club president and explained my situation and told her I would not be at the meeting, but I would be at the next one. She called a week ahead of time to remind me, and I reluctantly committed to going to the November meeting. I was still grieving.

It was the day of the meeting, and I was having second thoughts. I didn't feel very sociable but thought how nice it would be to help others and not dwell on my situation. The meeting was in a small room at Hillcrest, a retirement facility. I entered the room. Again I didn't know any of the other ladies. I put on my best smile and introduced myself to everyone at my table. Sitting next to me was Barbara. She was very friendly, close to my age, probably younger. She told me she lived in San Dimas, and we talked about why we joined.

"I had a hard time coming to the meeting tonight," I told her. "My husband of fifty-eight years just passed away last month. I came tonight because I think it's important to stay active, to keep my mind off the fact that my husband was gone."

"I know," she replied. "My husband just passed away six months ago." We shared with each other how our husband's had passed and the feelings we were experiencing.

Did God sit us next to each other? I wondered. *I believe that things happen for a reason and we both needed a friend.*

Barbara and I have become good friends. She was married to Dan for fifty years. "We shared everything with each other," she told me. "We had the same goals in life and separately we were strong. Dan had cancer for years, but I didn't know it until six weeks before he passed. Why didn't he tell me I wondered? At first I was angry, and then I realized he just wanted to keep things normal. He was afraid if the kids and I knew we would hover over him, and he didn't want pity or to see the sadness in our eyes. I thought I was so independent, but now I don't even know who I am without him."

She said there were times she obsessed about death. Like me, she wondered how much time she had left.

"Sometimes I wonder how long I might lay on my second story stairwell before anyone would find me?" she said.

"I pray every night, 'Please, God, don't let my kids find me dead in this bed.'" Not because I was afraid to die, but it would be too much for my children and grandchildren to bear after losing their Dad and Papa.

"I didn't expect that so many things that made me happy around the house now make me sad and are painful reminders that Dan is dead, and I am now identified as a widow!"

I know there are many widows in the world. *Did their hearts hurt as much as Barbara's and mine?* I wondered. I feel ashamed that I didn't spend more time with my mother after my father died. He was only sixty-years-old. I never asked her how she was doing. I was busy working and with my husband and raising our two children. My dad had been sick for a year, and we knew the end was near.

I was sad and emotional as I helped her make arrangements for his funeral. *Was she broken inside? Did she feel totally lost like I do? Shame on me for not asking.*

Barbara told me how she strategized to deal with and to combat with her flood of emotions. "I talked about Dan with my family and friends even when they tried to change the subject, seeing the tears flowing down my checks. If I don't keep his memory alive will he disappear?"

She told me she put together a written summary on who he was, his accomplishments, and how much he meant to her. She wanted the great-grandchildren not even born yet, to know who he was. That made me think about the five book series I just finished. I didn't realize at the time I was writing a blueprint of my childhood and the early years of my married life with Randall.

"Did you go to any grief counseling?" I asked her.

"Yes. I was sure the experts could help me get through this tough time, and then I realized I was an expert on grief. I felt almost worse after a session over the pain of the other participants so I soon stopped going. I read books on grief and self-help but ended up feeling unhappy. The most helpful book was, "All The Light We Cannot See." It asked the question, 'Don't you Want To Live Before You Die?'"

We both push ourselves to keep busy and to keep our minds in a positive flow. Here are a few things Barbara shared with me how she helped to energize herself and keep happy:

- Keeping busy to energize myself or someone else or a cause. Choosing activities that made me happier. I forced myself to do things around the house that I had been putting off for years
- I bought myself flowers every once in a while, and I still wear Dan's favorite gray shorts.
- I would go outside and walk or work to enjoy the sunrise/sunset, or just breathe, slowly and deeply.
- I added a yoga class to my routine. I needed its healthful "Attitude adjustment" to live in the present moment, re-noticing the world with curiosity and acceptance.
- I bought a wind chime whose delicate lilt brought me peace and pleasure.
- I was grateful for all the memories and experience of my life and even the fact that Dan went first. I would not wish the pain and trouble that I was going through on him.
- I started journaling, something I had never done before. The exercise and reflection felt cathartic. Maybe because I now have perspective.
- I made new friends and traveled with old ones.
- Every day I tried to add beauty around myself, inside and outside the house. I discriminately got rid of whatever just "sat around."
- I learned something new. I started with the four TV remotes and the lawn's sprinkler timer. (Barbara told me she thought she set the sprinkler to go on at ten in the evening. But instead, she set it to run for ten straight hours.)

- For the first time I put together a 1000 piece puzzle. It taxed my patience but kept my mind occupied and gave my brain and heart a break.
- Gardening was never my strong suit, but now I grow things, nurture them and even talk to them. I have developed a renewed appreciation for all things living.
- Daily I look for an *AWE* moment.
- I replaced my king-size mattress, which was so big, cold and made me feel lonely, with a queen-size mattress.
- I joined a club that volunteers (GFWC La Verne-San Dimas Woman's Club) to reach out and help others in need. And do something for someone else.

Words from Barbara: Dan's death has taught me how woefully inadequate I have been over the years in addressing other people's losses. I now speak and behave a little differently: for example, instead of saying, "Please let me know if there is anything I can do." I say, "What can I do to help you today?"

I don't envision marrying again, and maybe not even falling in love again, but I do keep an open mind and an open heart to all possibilities. Even though I still see and hear Dan every day, each day I smile more. Time really does help heal….

I want to thank Barbara for being my friend when I needed it the most. She was someone who certainly knew the feelings I was experiencing.

TEN

Randall loved Las Vegas. In our early married years, the 50s, we often went there with no more than a $100. *We couldn't do that today.* Before he passed, we would go four to five times a year. We went often enough that our hotel stay was free and we received complimentary invitations to top entertainers' show, such as; Cher, Elton John, Tony Bennett and Lady Gaga, and Rod Stewart to name a few.

The last time we were there we saw the coming attraction posters for Jennifer Lopez. He pointed out the poster at Caesars' Palace. "That is one show I want to see. I hope we get tickets the first of the year," he said. Sure enough in January, because it was his birthday month, the invitation came in the mail. It was only right that I go, but the invite was directed to Randall.

I called Mindy and told her, "I just got an invitation to Jennifer Lopez's show in Vegas. If I can work something out, will you go with me?"

"Absolutely, yes!" she said.

"I might have to tell a little white lie. Do you think Dad would mind?"

"If it gets us in the show, it's okay."

I hung up the phone and thought about how I was going to make that happen.

***

WHAT THE HELL JUST HAPPENED?

I sat by the telephone with the invitation to the Jennifer Lopez Concert in one hand and Randall's player card in the other. I decided to give the casino a call.

"Hello. Welcome to Caesar's Entertainment," said the operator.

"Hello. This is Mrs. Miller, and I would like to activate the invitation to the Jennifer Lopez concert we received."

"One moment, and I'll connect you."

"Hello," said the next operator. "Welcome to Caesar's Player Club. Who am I speaking with?"

Okay, here it goes. "I'm Tamara Miller, and my husband and I received an invitation to the Jennifer Lopez concert. My husband, Jack Miller is at work and asked me to call and reserve our spot for the concert."

"What is the code number on the invitation?"

I gave her the number. She asked what night we would like to come. I gave her the dates for a two-night stay. She read back the confirmation and said she would be sending me an email.

"Thank you for calling Caesar's Players' Club. Enjoy the concert."

"Thank you," I said and hung up the phone. That was too easy, and I did feel a little guilty; just a little guilty. But not enough to explain to them he was working in Heaven not on Earth. I called Mindy and told her to start packing; we were going to Las Vegas.

***

I had his Players' Card with me when we checked in, plus the invitation and Randall's death certificate. I explained to the booking agent that my husband had recently passed away, hoping they would not look at the date. Going to the computer, the agent pulled up my reservation. He looked at the invitation, and then the death certificate. He excused himself and disappeared to the back room.

This isn't going to work, I thought. *I've been busted.*

I looked at Mindy, and whispered, "I think we might be in trouble here. In case we get thrown out, we'll go to another casino and I'll pay for the room. We'll just have a weekend in Vegas." We waited for about ten minutes.

The agent returned. He handed me back the death certificate. "I'm sorry for you lose, but you understand this invitation is in your husband's name. We will still compensate your room, but not your tickets to the concert."

"I realize the invitation is in his name, but the points on the card are a combination of his and mine too," I said.

"We don't know that."

"You can look at all our previous reservations, and see that we were here together, and that I did not have a separate card."

"I'm sorry Mrs. Miller but we have rules to follow, which at this point is related to Mr. Miller's participation."

"May I speak to the Casino Manager?"

"Certainly. Please wait over there," he told us, referring to an area away from the reception counter.

I had previously met the Casino Manager Vinny, but didn't think he would remember me. He greeted me, and I explained the situation to him. I even showed him a picture of Randall on my cell phone, hoping he would remember him. On many of our visits, he had approached us with a warm welcome.

It didn't work. He took my tickets to Jennifer Lopez. *What a hard-hearted man.*

"That's okay," I told Mindy. "Let's go to the ticket desk. I'll pay for them. I don't care how much it costs. I guess that's the price I pay for lying."

When we got to the Ticket Master, we were told they were all sold out. I tried to explain to them that I knew there were two tickets available, because I just had my tickets taken away.

"I'm sorry," said the ticket agent. "Those are comp tickets, and I can't access them."

"Is there a waitlist in case of any cancellations?" I asked.

"I'm sorry, but no."

I walked away, not knowing if I was going to cry or lose my temper. "I need a drink," I told Mindy, and we headed for the bar. I called Cory to vent about what had just happened.

"So what are we going to do with the rest of our time?" I asked Mindy, as we sipped on our drink. We came up with a few ideas, but nothing special. "Mindy, have you ever been to a psychic?"

"No. Let's do it! Maybe we could talk to Dad," she said, with a laugh. She got on the internet on her phone and found a medium at the Palms Casino. She called her, and we made an appointment for two o'clock.

We arrived at the Palms and found the medium located in a small alcove, not much bigger than a closet. Mindy and I were both nervous. The woman looked just like any other woman. I don't know what I was expecting. Maybe someone with a lot of makeup surrounded by many candles and satanic music.

She asked us to take a seat and then pulled a curtain to separate us from the casino. We were both skeptical, and I listened for things she would say that were too generic.

"Why are you here to see me today?" she asked.

"My husband recently passed away, and I wondered if you can tell me anything about him?" I told her.

The woman closed her eyes and moved her right hand in a circle over her chest. "It was a heart attack," she said. *It was something like a heart attack,* I thought. "It happened in your home." She opened her eyes and looked at me for confirmation. I nodded and started to cry. *The front room of our mobile home did look like our home.*

"I see a brown chair," she continued. *That was the recliner he was sitting on when he died.* "He said to tell you there was nothing you could have done. He wants you to know that. It happened so fast, and he was not in any pain." Mindy and I were both crying now. "He is saying something about flowers."

I was not sure what that meant, only that his yard was so important to him. Maybe he wanted me to be sure that I took good care of it.

She started talking again. "I see him with a younger man. Is there someone who has recently passed?"

"His friend from work, Reuben, but he is older," I responded. I looked at Mindy, and she couldn't think of anyone. "The wife of one of our close friend's passed away in January."

"No, it's a male," she responded. She looked at her watch and said our time was up. I had only paid for thirty minutes. The time went fast, and it was a very emotional experience. We thanked her and left.

As we walked to the car, I looked at Mindy and said, "It was Jeff. That's who was the younger man with Dad!"

"You're right! That was who it was."

Randall's brother had a son named Jeff. He had passed away in December. That made sense.

When we got back to our room I called Cory to tell him about the physic. He found it interesting but was a little skeptical.

"Mom, my boss, Tom Pena was telling me he needed to call Vegas to make his reservation for the Super Bowl," said Cory. "I told him about the problem you had with the tickets to Jennifer Lopez. He picked up the phone and made a call. He said to tell you to go to 'Will Call', your tickets are waiting."

"What? But they are all sold out."

"Tom made a call. That's all I know."

"Wow, I can't believe it. Tom has people!"

"I guess he does," said Cory.

"That is so exciting. I still can't believe it. I can't wait to tell Mindy. Tell Tom I love him. Talk with you later. Bye."

When I told Mindy, she couldn't believe it either. We went to the show that night, and it was fantastic. The seats were better than the comp ones. It felt like Randall was there with us. What an amazing day.

WHAT THE HELL JUST HAPPENED?

Once we returned home and told the family about meeting with the physic in Vegas, Tonya, my oldest granddaughter, wanted to experience it too. She went on the internet and found a medium in Santa Ana.

Almost everyone in the family wanted to go. In checking her website, she was having a group meeting in March. Her group meetings consisted of ten people, which were about two hours long. Tonya, Mindy, her husband Darren, Cory's girlfriend, and I made reservations. I was excited to experience a connection with Randall again.

€

We had a Family Trust. After Randall's death, I called the attorney to see if I needed to do anything or sign any paperwork. He said because I was listed as Trustee, there was nothing I had to do. He said I was now in charge of all the assets.

During the last six months, I had received a massive amount of paper work related to Randall's death. If I hadn't had some business sense, I would have sat at the kitchen table crying out of frustration. I was glad I order twelve original death certificates, fifteen might have been better. If an original was not required, I gave them a copy.

We both had 401K's which amounted to double the amount of forms. It took several mailings to get the name changed and listing new beneficiaries. We had two boats with trailers, two cars, and a mobile home. Then there were bank and household accounts, not to mention credit cards. Cancelling accounts could not be done over the phone. Written requests were usually needed, along with a death certificate. Changing everything to my name seemed like an endless job.

ELEVEN

Life was settling down for me. I had been back to the river several times with my daughter and son-in-law since Randall passed. They both work, so our trips were usually only weekends. I wanted to spend a whole week there.

Randall never let me go alone because he worried for my safety on a four-hour drive through the desert. Of course, my two children were the ones who were worried about me now, but I convinced them that I would call from my cell phone when I made two stops at rest areas on the way.

I love our river home. It has so many wonderful memories. Getting ready for the trip was more difficult than I thought. Randall and I had shared duties getting the car packed before and now it was all my responsibility. Doing it alone, I was concerned I would forget something. I put Kissy in the car, and we were on our way.

Pulling into the mobile park my heart started to race and an uncontrollable flood of tears covered my face. Walking inside, the first thing I saw was his recliner where I had found him unresponsive. I curled up on it and had a total meltdown.

Taking a deep breath, I told myself I had to be a big girl and get a hold of my emotions. I unpacked the car and took Kissy for a walk along the river.

***

The next morning the sun was shining and the warmth felt good on my body, as I had my coffee on the porch, spending my first day there alone as a widow. Life would never be the same again, but that didn't mean I had to stop living.

It was mid-week, so the park was almost empty. A young man and his dog lived in the trailer next to me. He was a worker in the park.

As I enjoyed my second cup of coffee, a young girl came out of a trailer across from me, pushing a stroller with a baby. She smiled and I smiled back with a 'good morning' greeting.

I saw a man leaving their trailer. I assumed he was her husband.

Needing some groceries, I drove thirty minutes into town to do a little shopping. Returning home, I put my groceries away and then took Kissy for a short walk. I sat on my porch with a cold drink and my Kindle on which I had downloaded several books. It was time to catch up on my reading.

I had only read one chapter when the young woman approached me, pushing her stroller. We introduced ourselves. She said her name was Sky. She told me she was a descendant of one of the local Indian tribes.

"Are you going to town today?" Sky asked me. "I'm out of diapers and wondered if you could buy some for me?"

"I just went to the store this morning. I'm sorry."

"My friend has gone to work and won't be back until tonight. I only have two diapers left."

Friend? I thought. *I guess he's not her husband.* Sky just stood there as if she was thinking about her dilemma.

I really don't have anything planned today, I thought. *I should give her a ride to the store. I remember being a young mother and all the worries that came with having a small child.*

"I will take you to the store," I offered.

"I hate to bother you, but I would appreciate it," said Sky.

"Let me know when you are ready."

"If we can go now, I'll just get my purse and the car seat."

"Yes, that will be fine."

Five minutes later, I met her at my car. "This is really a nice Mercedes," she said as she hooked the car seat in the back. She buckled her one-year-old little boy in place, and we put the stroller in the trunk.

Strangely, she got in the back seat next to her boy.

"Don't you want to sit up front?" I asked.

"No. I like to sit by my baby," replied Sky.

I guess that's okay, I thought. I was just uncomfortable having her sit in back of me.

As I pulled out of the park onto the main street, I asked, "Do you want to go to Wal-Mart or the grocery store?"

"If you don't mind, I need to make a stop at my girlfriend's house. She owes me money, and I only have food stamps. She lives at the Blue Water mobile home park with her dad. It's on the way."

Oh no, I thought. *Her story is already changing. I don't know this girl. Have I made a mistake by helping her?*

I made small talk as we drove. It was about fifteen minutes to the Blue Water Park. I was getting a little nervous, and my mind started wandering. *She is sitting in the back seat and probably has a gun in her diaper bag. She is going to shoot me in the head, take all my money, and steal my car. My kids will never find my body. Oh stop it! You have been watching too many Lifetime movies,* I told myself.

"Which trailer does your friend live in?" I asked, as we entered the park.

"Just go to the end of the street and make a right," Sky said.

When I turned, she said, "I thought it was here, but I guess we are on the wrong street. Make a left up there." She pointed out the direction.

My heart was racing, and I had worked myself into what my grandmother called a 'tizzy'. *She probably took me here to make a drug deal. I think I'll tell her we are going home.*

"Pull up where the red mailbox is. I think that's her place," directed Sky. When I stopped the car she said, "No, that's not it."

WHAT THE HELL JUST HAPPENED?

"Okay, Sky. This is what we are going to do. I'm going to give you ten dollars, and I'll take you to the store to get your diapers, and then we're going home," I said in my best take charge voice. I hoped she didn't notice it quivering because now I was a little scared, at the same time thinking she could shoot me in the head. I didn't like that she was sitting in the back seat. Was I overreacting?

"I appreciate that," said Sky as I handed her ten dollars and drove toward the market. Parking in the Safeway lot, Sky got out of the car. "I'll be right back," she said.

Her baby is asleep. I guess that's why she didn't take him, I thought. *She doesn't know me but trusted leaving him in my care. I'm just being silly? I'll be home soon and will consider this a lesson learned. I hope my kids never find out what I have done. They'll never let me come to the river alone again.*

I saw her diaper bag on the back seat. I couldn't help myself. I checked it to make sure she didn't have a gun tucked away. I felt a little ridiculous as I went through it, but was relieved that I didn't find one.

Ten more minutes passed, and my mind took off again. *Sky thinks I am rich because I am driving a Mercedes and that I'm a nice lady. She has decided to leave her baby with me to raise.*

I'll give her five more minutes, and then I'll go inside the store and look for her. If I don't find her I'll take her baby to the police station. I sure have gotten myself in a mess. Then I saw her running from the store carrying about eight grocery bags.

Of course, the first thing that crossed my mind was that she had run out without paying, and I am now the get-away driver. Nearing the car she slowed down, and I was relieved that I didn't see anyone chasing her.

"I'm so sorry it took me so long," she said, slightly out of breath. "While I was in the store I thought I would buy what I needed with my food stamps."

I was so relieved that I couldn't put her groceries in the trunk fast enough. I don't know what she had planned, but we were going straight home. I was a little embarrassed that I let my mind get so carried away.

We were home! I helped her unload her groceries. Her baby was still asleep. She thanked me, and I said, "No problem." I locked my car and returned to the safety of my mobile home.

It took me a while to calm down. I couldn't believe how upset I got. I promised myself, no more helping people I don't know.

The next morning, I was having my coffee inside. For some reason I didn't want to go outside. Someone knocked on my door. It was Sky.

"Good morning," I greeted her.

"Sorry to bother you again, but could you give me a ride to my brother's house. He's not too far from here."

"I'm sorry, Sky. I really can't, I have a lot to do today." Just a little white lie.

"I don't know what to do. My friend said I have to get out of his house. He said if I didn't put out, I needed to get out. I thought he was a friend. Boy was I wrong."

"If he wants you out, can't he take you to your brother's?"

"He said he wouldn't. He had to go to work."

"I can call the park manager and see if they have another mobile where you can stay in." *This should not be my problem*, I thought. *Her friend works for the park, let them straighten it out.*

"Thanks. I appreciate your help. I'll check back with you later," she said and left.

I called the park manager and told them what Sky had said. I probably got him in trouble because he let someone live with him. The manager said he would take care of it.

Still afraid to go outside, I sat on my couch, which faced their trailer directly, and waited to see if he left or took her somewhere. In about an hour, I saw the two of them with the baby leave. I sighed in relief, hoping everything was handled.

I tried to watch television to get my mind off Sky and her friend. But it didn't work. I soon saw the man come back to the trailer, alone.

He had a little dog and took him out for a minute and then looked toward my trailer. Like I said, my front room looked directly at his mobile.

How come he is not at work? Did they fire him? I wondered. *Oh no, is he mad at me now?*

Again, my mind took off into the unknown. *He is going to break into my trailer tonight and kill me!* I looked at my little dog and said, "Kissy, I'm packing up, and we are going home." And, that is just what I did.

€

Driving home I realized how safe I always felt with Randall. One of those things you take for granted until your world is shaken upside down. When he went on fishing trips and I was home alone, I never was scared. After he passed away I worried about someone coming into the house at night. I would hear noises, and if Kissy barked, I would get up to see what had alarmed her. It was always nothing. I finally had an alarm installed in the house. That really helped.

TWELVE

The night finally came when we went to see the psychic medium in Santa Ana. (For the purpose of this writing, I will refer to her as Mary) I'm anxious. There was no guarantee that I will be able to connect with Randall. Our group will consist of my daughter, Mindy, her husband, Darren, my granddaughter Tonya, and me. Cory and his girlfriend will meet us there. Cory didn't want to be part of the group. He said he would wait outside. *Chicken!* Other than my family there would be five other guests.

The medium was located in a commercial complex, where we all met outside. Mindy and I are the only ones who had experienced a session with a medium before. I wondered if this will be the same as the one in Las Vegas.

Darren told Cory, "I can't believe that I let these girls talk me into this."

"Are you a believer?" asked Cory.

"Not really, but I'm curious enough to see what will happen."

Entering the meeting reception area, we were greeted by the medium's assistant. We were instructed to select a random card from a tarot deck and then take a seat in the meeting room. There were ten chairs in a semi-circle with one chair facing the circle.

The medium came in and introduced herself. She asked each of us to read aloud our cards. She told me my card was Fiona, the oracle angel. The medium explained that Fiona was watching me struggle and would help me through it.

WHAT THE HELL JUST HAPPENED?

Tonya's card was the Archangel Michael, the chief of angels. She explained he was the angel of protection. She told her he would protect her, and give her the courage and strength to deal with the crisis she was facing. Each person read their card as the medium gave her interpretation of the meaning. We then took a ten-minute break.

When we all returned, the lighting in the room was dim. Mary told us that during the reading not to give her any names or hints unless she asked. She would work through it, finding the right connection. She would give a person's initial or sound out a name. If we gave her a name, it might take her to the wrong person.

Mary sat with her eyes closed. She had a pad and pencil on her lap, and sometimes she would write something down. Other times it looked like she was just drawing circles.

Still with her eyes closed, she said she was receiving a "J" and a "K" sound. "Is there a Jack?" She opened her eyes and looked for some acknowledgement.

My daughter raised her hand. "My dad's name is Jack, but he went by his middle name, Randall."

"He is really talkative," she said. She looked at Cory's girlfriend. "Are you dating his son?" She acknowledged with a nod. "He says you are good for him, and he is good for you."

That is true, I thought.

"He is proud of his son," she continued. "They are good together." She looked at Tonya. "How are your related?"

"I'm his granddaughter," said Tonya.

"He sees you crying and that you are having a hard time. He said to tell you he was not afraid of death, that he had a good life. He was a good man. Boy he's a Chatty Kathy! He has so much to say." She was making a motion with her hand in a circle in front of her chest. "Did he die of a heart attack?"

"It was a blood clot to his heart that went to his brain," I responded.

The medium continued. "He did not know what happened," she said looking at me. "He hadn't been feeling well, but didn't think it was important. I see him in your front room on a brown chair, and a dog is there. He saw you lift him onto the floor and do compressions on his chest, he felt your panic. He remembered the ride in the ambulance, and he stayed around for a few days. I see him as his younger self, 35-40 years old." Mary laughed. "He said that was when he was most handsome. He knows you miss him. He said he should have been more romantic. Was he romantic?"

"Not really," I said.

"He said to remind you that he did buy you jewelry," she said.

"Yes, he did." I replied. *That made the family laugh, because they knew that was the way he made up to me if I was mad at him.*

"He mentions the dog a lot," she said. "He said to keep the blanket and the dog on the bed. He said the dog sees him and they play together in the backyard. He watches you in the kitchen. He likes your baking. Is there a table in the kitchen area?" she asks me.

"Yes," I said.

"He sits there and watches you." The medium paused and pointed to the area between where Tonya and I were sitting. "I see him standing there behind the two of you." Tonya and I looked at each other, as tears flooded our faces. "He has a child with him. One whose feet have not touched the earth." She paused. "Did you have a child that died?" she asked me.

"Yes. We had a child that lived for five hours," I answered.

"Your baby is with him." That sent me on an emotional tidal wave and pushed me over the edge. "He said you are happy at your house, and you should stay there. He said you can get rid of his clothes, but save two hats," she laughed, "and one pair of underwear?"

That had meaning to me, because he had a lot of baseball caps at the river, and two were his favorites. At the river I found a pair of his underpants under our bed. I took it home and washed it. On the next trip back, I put the pants back under the bed. I thought that might keep him close when I was there.

"He said to tell you he liked the guy who did the eulogy. He told funny stories. You know he is not at the cemetery, but he sees you when you are there." She looked at all of us. "He is not going to stop talking. I'm going to have to tell him good-bye, because I need to get to the others that are here."

Before he left, he spoke through Mary to Mindy, on how proud he was of her and how much he loved her. "You really need to have a private reading," she told me. "I can't get him to quit talking." She waved her hand again as if to dismiss him.

Next Darren's mother came through. The medium made several comments from his mother that was spot on. He was stunned. He's not a skeptic anymore. She continued to address the rest of the guests. You could tell by the responses she received from them, that a loved one had come through to talk to each one.

As emotional as it was, it gave me a sense of comfort. I wanted to hear more. The following month, I called and set up an appointment for her to come to my house for a private reading. She said I could also invite a few other guests.

My granddaughter, Darriana did not get to go with us to Mary's first reading, because she had to work. I scheduled the meeting on her day off.

Tonya wanted to ask about the flickering of lights at her house, and about her five- year- old daughter who was talking to someone in the hall and in her bedroom. When Tonya asked her daughter who she was talking to, she said it was a man, but not Randall.

Darriana wanted to reach out to him. She was getting married in October and was looking forward to a special dance with her Papa. They had talked about their dance together before he passed.

Mary said he would be there. Something would happen at the reception or during the ceremony to let her know he was there.

I had several incidents that happened during the night that I had not told anyone. Was I dreaming? Or did Randall visit me?

One night when I was sleeping on my side, I woke up because I felt something pressing against my back. At first I thought maybe it was my dog, Kissy lying next to me. I rolled over to check, but nothing was there.

A few nights later, I woke with a start and saw Randall above me with his arms stretched out to me. I called his name and he disappeared as if going through me.

Are these things happening because I went to the medium? If so, I hope he comes to me again.

€

Once again, this was another hard chapter to write. I had to refer to my journal to refresh myself what I had gone through at the time. As far as the meeting with the medium, you could find things that might be generic, like watching me in the kitchen, being proud of our children, seeing us cry, missing us, and playing with the dog. But then again, she mentioned incidents that no one knew about.

Mary did not know how Randall died, or where it happened. I believe he did stay around for several days while we were at the hospital. I remember small signs that told me he was still there with us. But when she said she saw him with our baby, how would she know that? That made a true believer out of me.

What about the pair of underpants? How did she know about that? He had to have told her. I can't wait to see Mary again.

THIRTEEN

I couldn't get the experience with the medium off my mind. I wondered if Randall would still visit me and if he was watching over me. I was so moved by what Mary said. There were times when I watched Kissy in the back yard for any indication that he was around,

Four months after Randall's passing his brother came for a visit. Whenever he sat in Randall's chair, Kissy would run to him and want to be picked up. Was it the chair, his brother, or was Randall with us?

Several times I had difficulty finding things where I had left them. I chalked it up to my state of confusion. Then I remembered Mary telling me that I might find things in my house moved. She said that was Randall letting me know he was still around. I wanted so much to believe that.

I called Mary to set up a private meeting in my home. She said she did make house visits if that was what I was interested in, and I could have up to six guests. I called three of my friends and asked if they would be interested in attending.

Sally– A long-time friend who I had worked with and who previously consulted a medium, and was excited to attend.

Barbara – She was someone who I had recently met whose husband had passed away six months before Randall. I had shared with her my experience with the medium. At first she was not too sure about the whole thing, but decided to come.

Carol – Another friend who I had previously worked with and who had become my dearest friend, she was open to the experience.

Of course, my daughter Mindy, along with my two granddaughters, Tonya and Darriana would be there.

***

All my guests had arrived and were waiting for Mary. We talked about what to expect. Sally was hoping to connect with her brother. Barbara was hoping to connect with her past husband. Carol was open. My family and I were hoping to hear from Randall again.

Both my parents were deceased, and tried to come through on my last visit with Mary. She said the initial of their first names and sounded out a name that I recognized as my father, and then my mother. But Randall had taken up so much time she had to dismiss them. Mary told us she had no control over who would come forward.

The doorbell rang. I could feel my heart in my throat. I opened the door, and, the minute I saw Mary, the tears started to flow. The thought of hearing from Randall again was overwhelming. She entered; I hugged her and felt an electrifying sensation go through my body. Her assistant was with her. She apologized for being late, but the traffic from Los Angeles was more than she had anticipated. Later I found out that Mary never drives herself, because the voices and images that came through were too much of a distraction.

I introduced Mary and her assistant to my group of family and friends. We all took a seat in the front room. She spread out the tarot cards on my coffee table, and we each took one at random. I don't remember what mine was, just that it was appropriate to what I had been going through.

Mary told us that she had been locked in a refrigerator when she was a young girl, and close to death when they found her. The spirits have been with her ever since, and she has had many talks with her father after he passed away. He told her what Heaven was like.

After reading the tarot cards we took a short break and then returned to the front room to see if any of us would receive a connection.

Mary said an initial and then a name. It was acknowledged by Sally. It was her father. She had two brothers; and her father acknowledged he had been very hard on her and apologized for favoring the boys. He said he hadn't been fair to her and was sorry for that. He said that he loved her very much and was proud of her. Mary went into details about several incidents where he had not been fair. Sally acknowledged everything Mary said and was astonished that the comments were right on.

Barbara was hoping to connect with her husband. Instead her younger sister came through. She was surprised about the loving comments her sister said because they had not been close. Mary started humming a song. "Do you recognize that?" she asked.

"Yes," responded Barbara. "That's a song' my sister always sang."

Carol's mother came through, and tears immediately formed in her eyes. She loved her mother and missed her very much. Carol had been raised on a farm. Mary described her house to a tee. She described the color of the house, the walkway, the porch, and the pots of flowers in the front of the house.

"One more thing," said Mary. "Your mother always carried a hanky in her bra."

Carol reached in her bra and pulled out a hanky, just like her mother.

"I see a lot of water," said Mary. Carol then told about a flood at her home when she was a girl.

Mary turned her comments to Mindy. Randall had a message for her, which she relayed to her. It was personal, so I'm not sharing that conversation.

She then looked at Darriana. "I'm getting married in October. I was going to have a special dance with my Papa." She started to tear up. "Do you think he will be there?"

"Yes," said Mary. "Watch for a sign. A flashing light, a crash, or loud noise. He will let you know he is there."

Tonya told Mary, "My six year-old daughter, Laney has been talking to someone in the hallway, and we recently moved into a new house and there are flickering lights. I asked her if it was her Papa. She said it wasn't. It is really making me feel uneasy."

Mary asked for her address and said she would drive by.

Mary then looked at me and closed her eyes, as if deep in thought. She opened her eyes and said, "You felt something press on your back during the night. You thought it was a dream. It wasn't. He was with you." She paused. "He came to you during the night. He reached out to you. You called his name, and he disappeared. You thought it was a dream, it wasn't." *How could she know that?* I wondered. *I hadn't told anyone.*

"Yes, that happened," I acknowledged. "I want him to come again."

"He's really busy," she answered.

"Doing what?" I asked rather loudly.

"My father explained to me that once in Heaven you have assignments," said Mary. "One of the duties is being a greeter. It is your job to be there to meet your family and friends when they arrive. My father also told me you have to get used to your heavenly body and learn how to get around. They reappear to their love ones usually within the first thirty to sixty days following their passing."

"Well, tell him I want him to visit me again," I told her. She was sitting next to some pictures I had on several tables, which had been taken in the last three years. "That is what Randall looks like," I said, pointing to the pictures.

She turned and glanced at the pictures, and said, "That's not how I see him. I see him much younger."

I had heard that once in Heaven you returned to your personal best.

WHAT THE HELL JUST HAPPENED?

Mary had completed a reading for everyone and her time was up. She thanked us for having her and wished us all peace.

***

We all gathered in the kitchen after Mary left. My guests were amazed at the accuracy of what she had told them. It is something we will talk about for days, or years, to come.

After the last session with Mary I began to wonder what Heaven was like. What do you do once you get there? No one has returned from Heaven to tell us about what goes on once you arrive. I had heard stories about some who had crossed over during a major surgery or a tragic accident and came back to tell about their experience.

I found a few books that had been written about such cases. One was "Imagine Heaven", written by John Burke, about doctors who had interviewed their patients who had crossed over, and told what they saw and how they felt. In reading their stories I was reminded of an incident that happened to my mother. I will share it with you in my next chapter.

€

After Mary left my home, she drove by Tonya's house. She later called Tonya and told her that there was a man's spirit present who had previously lived there. She said she sent him away. After the drive by, Tonya's daughter ceased talking to him. But there were still flickering lights.

At Darriana's wedding, during a speech she and her husband were thanking everyone for joining them at this special occasion, a light above their heads burst. Was it Randall? We would like to think so, but who knows?

FOURTEEN

The holidays were approaching, and it had been a little over a year since Randall had passed away. The first holidays were rough. This one should be a little easier, although it will never be the same.

It was early morning, and I was fixing my first cup of coffee when the phone rang. *It is too early for any of the family to be calling,* I thought.

"Hello?" I said.

"Tami. It's Carole."

Carole and her husband Jack had been friends of Randall's since grammar school. They were the first couple I met when I started dating him. I knew Carole's voice, but something about the tone was different.

"Hi, Carole."

"Jack's dead! Vanessa found him on his chair this morning, dead," she blurted out through sobs.

"I'll be right there," I said and hung up. There was no time to ask questions. I felt this friend needed me right away. She lived in Chino, about thirty minutes away. I pulled on some sweatpants and sweatshirt. No time for make-up. I felt an urgency to get to her as soon as possible.

I didn't see any cars in front of her house. It appeared that no one else was there yet. I knocked on her door. Vanessa, Carole's daughter answered.

"Vanessa, I'm so sorry," I said as I reached out to give her a hug.

"Mom's in here," she said, and I followed her.

Carole had circulation problems and other health issues due to smoking most of her young life. She was sitting in her wheelchair next to the kitchen table. I put my arms around her, and we sobbed together. Vanessa handed us some Kleenex as our crying slowly subsided.

"Many nights Jack fell asleep in his chair watching television too tired to get up and come to bed," said Carole. "When Vanessa woke up this morning, thinking her dad was asleep as he lay on the couch, she touched his shoulder to wake him. He didn't move. She screamed for me. I was already getting up and in the process of coming to the family room."

"I can't wake Dad up," Vanessa yelled. "Mom, I can't wake him up!"

"I told her to call 911," said Carole. "Just in case he might only be unconscious. When the paramedics arrived, they pronounced him dead immediately and called the mortuary to come and get his body. Time went by so fast, but, at the same time, so slow."

"This is so hard to believe," I said. "Jack was the healthiest out of all the guys. He exercised and swam almost every day."

She had already called her two other daughters and was waiting for them to get there. We periodically cried and then laughed as we remembered stories about how much trouble Jack and Randall had gotten into in their early years.

"Just two weeks ago, I was in the hospital," said Carole. "I was having a problem breathing, among some other issues. I was there over three weeks. At one time I was on life support and there was some discussion about pulling the plug; Jack was furious. He said, 'No way. She will come out of this. We are about to have our sixtieth wedding anniversary and Carole would not miss that for anything.' I should be the one dead, not him." Carole was in a wheelchair due to previously having her leg amputated.

She was probably thinking, *What will I do now?* Jack did the shopping, cooking, bill paying, caring for Carole's needs, and driving her from place to place. Of course I didn't know her financial situation nor was this the time to ask.

Her two daughters arrived. Denise was the oldest and Tami a few years younger. They both grew up with my two children. It was good to see them again even under these circumstances. They both went to their mother, and they embraced and cried. It was time for me to leave.

"I'm going now, Carole. Please call me anytime you want to talk. I'll check back with you in a few days." We hugged and again started to cry. As I dried my eyes, Tami walked me to my car. We paused in the driveway and talked about the shock of losing her dad and the health issues her mother was having.

"Keep a close watch on your mother. It hasn't really hit her yet that she is on her own. This might send her over the edge and push her into depression. It's good that Vanessa lives with her. She won't have as much time to think. Also, get at least twelve to fifteen death certificates. She will need them to close out some business, and many items will require an original." I told her to call me anytime if I can help, and left.

***

After a few days, I called Carole to check on her. She seemed to be doing okay. But I thought she was probably not being truthful with herself or family. She said she liked to read, so I told her I would come by and bring her some books.

As I well knew, now that she was alone, she would be faced with many things and much business that needed to be taken care of. I didn't think this was the time to ask a lot of questions, or cross the personal line between her and her daughters.

The next day I took her some books to read. As we sat and visited, I asked if they had a family trust. She said no, they didn't even have a will. We talked about probate and the house. She indicated there wasn't any equity in the house and the bank was probably going to foreclose on it soon. She told me that Jack's older brother lived in the small house next door, which was on her property. He was retired and gave Jack his Social Security check each month. Jack paid all his household bills and many nights took him his meals. Now he would have to learn to live on his own.

From where we were sitting, I could see the backyard with a swimming pool. *Who was going to take care of all that now?* I wondered.

Jack had a small business, which his brother helped him run. That income was now gone. Carole and Jack both collected Social Security, but now she was entitled to only one, which would be Jack's because it was the larger of the two. There were three trucks in the driveway, which Carole could not drive and she wasn't sure where the ownership certificates were. Even if she had them how would she sell the vehicles? Vanessa had some health issues and never got a driver's license. She never needed one, because her dad took her anywhere she needed to go. Carole was unsure of their banking accounts, and definitely didn't know the password to get money from the ATM.

"Have you thought about when you will have Jack's service?" I asked.

Carole just shook her head. "I don't think I'll have one. He said he wanted to be cremated. I'll check and see what his sister and the girls want to do," she said, a little bewildered.

As I left, I reflected on how lucky I was. I had my health, and Randall left me financially sound. Yes, I struggled being alone and taking care of some of my new responsibilities. Later I will share with her some of the obstacles I faced, hoping it will help her get through the same.

***

A few weeks went by, and I went back to see how Carole was doing. She had handled many things by phone, and a friend had taken her to the Social Security office to inform them of Jack's death. Her son-in-law came weekly and took care of the yard work; he also was helping her sell the vehicles. Her finances were tight, and she was going to sell the house. Being in a wheelchair, the thought of getting the house ready was overwhelming. Her daughters and daughter-in-law helped with the preparation.

Carole wanted to get a small two-bedroom apartment, but what she found was out of her price range. She did find a one bedroom in an adult complex, but Vanessa did not meet the fifty-five-year-old age requirement. It was suggested that Carole could qualify having a caregiver. After further investigation, they filled out the necessary paperwork, and Vanessa qualified as her caregiver and was entitled for payment from the state.

Life was not easy for Carole, but she was determined to take care of herself. I wonder if I had been in Carole's situation if I would have done as well. She certainly is a survivor. I had some tough times but nothing like hers. I think Carole is the strongest woman I know.

FIFTEEN

Two years after Randall passed, I was feeling really sad. I wondered if that was what you feel like when you are depressed. I would pray at night for Randall to visit me. He didn't come. I guess he was too busy. I knew if I went to see Mary again I could talk to him through her. So I called her office and made an appointment. I wanted to ask if he saw me working in the yard? Did he know I was doing my best to keep things up?

Randall took so much pride in our backyard, and I didn't do yard work, or should I say, I didn't until it became my responsibility. We had a gardener, but Randall did most of the trimming. I found some hand clippers in our tool shed and started to whack away. There was also an electric hedge trimmer, but I had visions of losing control if I tried to use it. No telling what would happen.

***

Sitting in Mary's waiting room, I was feeling anxious. *Would I connect with him this time?* I wondered.

Mary welcomed me and we went into her office. She had a nice sitting area beside her desk. She didn't sit across her desk from me, she sat in a chair next to a love seat where I was sitting.

"How are you doing?' she asked.

"I've been feeling so sad and missing Randall," I said. "I thought if I came to you I could connect with him. I've been doing something that he would never expect me to do. I wondered if he knows."

She closed her eyes, and I waited.

"I see greenery and bushes," she said. "Are you planting flowers?"

"Yes, and I'm working in the yard, which is something I never did before."

"He knows, and is glad you are maintaining things." She paused. "You have done something to memorialize him."

I thought for a minute. *Memorialize him?* Then I remembered. "I placed a stone plaque where he had planted some bushes and a small tree. It reads: If tears could build a stairway and memories a lane, I'd walk right up to heaven and bring you home again."

"He said he likes that." She closed her eyes again. "He's talking about a Ja-Jac-Jack?"

"Randall's real name is Jack," I said.

"No, it's not him. Did a friend recently die with that name?"

"A year after Randall passed away, one of his best friends passed too. His name was Jack Garcia."

"They are together. Did he have a heart attack?"

"I don't know. His daughter found him deceased one morning on their couch."

"He had an embolism," said Mary. "There's a Ka-Ca?" Mary looked at me.

"His wife's name is Carol."

"Jack wants to thank you for being there for her. He appreciates the friendship you have given to her."

"Carol called me the morning after her daughter, who lives with them, found Jack on the couch. I dropped everything and drove to her house. It was about thirty minutes away. I stayed with her until her two other daughters got there. I knew what she was going through. We cried together."

Carol is faced with so many challenges. She is in a wheelchair and was dependent on Jack. Sometimes I feel guilty that I am so fortunate and count my blessing every day.

Mary was quiet for a minute. "Randall said to tell you he's glad you are still traveling. I'm getting an A sound, Ann? Are you going somewhere with Ann?"

"Anna! I'm going on a cruise with her next April." *Wow. Where did that come from?*

"He said that's good. You'll have fun together. He said he doesn't expect you to spend the rest of your life alone."

I laughed. "I don't believe that for one minute. He was a very jealous person."

"He said to tell you, that was then, this is now." *I still didn't believe it.*

Mary sat quietly for a minute and cocked her head as if she was listening to something. "I smell lemons," she said. "Do you have a lemon tree?"

"Yes, and it bears fruit almost all year round. All the kids come to pick them and take a bag home each time they come over."

"He sees them when they are at the lemon tree."

That made me cry but it also made me happy. "Does he see us when we go to his gravesite?"

"You know he is not there." she said. I nodded. "He knows when you visit." She stood up. I guessed that was a sign my session was over.

After I left her office, I sat in my car and wrote down everything she had told me, as I filtered through what she could have been guessing about and what was unknown. I thought it was strange that Jack came through. Either way, the visit was very comforting. I don't think I will need to go back again.

***

When I got home, I called Carol and told her what Mary had said about Jack. She was shocked and pleased at the same time, because she was not sure if Jack had had a heart attack or what had caused his death, because he had been so healthy. She found it interesting that Mary had identified it as an embolism, because Jack's sister had also had one, but she survived. She was glad that Jack and Randall were together. They had been good friends since grammar school.

***

I don't try to understand anything about the spirit world. I only know that the messages from Randall and my mother's experience were so real and gave me peace during my despondent hours. I can understand why someone would take measures to end it all when they are in so much pain and wanting to be with their loved one again, but the rest of the family are grieving too. I desperately wanted to be with Randall again and knew that would happen in the future. What was more important now was to be there for the younger ones left behind. My visits with Mary helped me through the grieving process.

€

My experiences with Mary were incredible. In the moment, it was overwhelming. We all still feel his presence from time to time. When something odd happens, we laugh and say, "That's Dad."

SIXTEEN

Previously I told you I would share the experience I had with my mother. Here it is;

Mother had been living at an Assisted Living facility, Sunrise Center, for over two years. A year ago, she needed more care and they moved her to another wing where care givers were there twenty-four hours. She had a blood disease that attacked her immune system, and she now was too weak to get out of bed on her own. Every day after work, for the past four months, I went to her room to help her eat dinner and to make sure she was doing okay.

On Friday evening when I arrived at Mother's, I knocked on her door. Her hearing is almost gone, so I didn't wait for a response, I was surprised to find Jan, her Hospice caregiver, sitting at her bedside.

"Is something wrong?" I asked.

"Your mother didn't wake up this afternoon so I was called. She seems to be resting peacefully, and her vitals are okay. She's in a deep sleep, semi-comatose; this sometimes happens. Let's step outside and talk."

My heart was beating fast; and I could feel my eyes tear up, as we stepped into the hallway.

"I think your Mother is near the end. She probably has about two weeks, at the most," said Jan.

I stood speechless for a moment. "This is hard to believe. I knew she was getting weaker, but I didn't expect anything like this so soon." We went back inside and I went directly to mother's bedside. I took her small frail hand in mine. "Mom, I'm here." She didn't respond. I wanted to have a chance to tell her good-bye, and to tell her how much I loved her.

Before Jan left, she said, "Call me if there is any change. I'll check back with you on Monday, if I don't hear from you during the weekend."

It seemed like such a short time ago that with perfect posture and head held high, the two of us walked through the large double doors of Sunrise Center. She nodded and greeted everyone. She was a little wobbly, but standing up straight, taking small steps she proudly entered as if she were a princess arriving to a grand ballroom.

How fast this past few years have slipped away, I thought.

I decided to wait until Monday to inform the family of mother's condition, in case Jan was wrong, and Mother woke up. I called my husband and he came right over. As I told him what Jan had said, he put his arms around me as I quietly broke down.

Later I called my boss and requested to take my two weeks' vacation, starting Monday. He understood and told me to take whatever time I needed. Mother slept the whole weekend, as I held vigilance over her.

Four days pass and Mother continued to sleep. Many times I stood by her bedside letting her know I was there. Her eyes seem to flicker under her eyelids, but they did not open.

It is now Tuesday morning, Mother is still asleep. I left to go to the main kitchen to get a cup of coffee and talk with a few of the other residents. They all wanted to know how Mother was doing. As I returned to her room I heard her calling my name.

"Mother, I'm here," I said, as I rushed to her bedside.

With outstretched arms she yells, "You found me! You found me!"

Bending over, I hugged her and held her tightly in my arms. She sobbed and seemed so frightened.

"I thought you would never come. I thought you would never find me," she whimpered. "They moved me to another room."

I explained to her she was still in the same room pointing out her furniture.

"You found me, so everything is okay now."

I just let it go; there was no sense dwelling on it. She was obviously confused. I nestled in bed next to her, and we lie quietly together for hours, as she fell in and out of sleep.

When Mother woke up again she told me she was hungry.

"Would you like me to get you some oatmeal?"

"Yes and some hot chocolate."

She's alive, and Jan was wrong. I was happy to get her anything she wanted.

I returned with her food. When she finished, she fell back to sleep, but this time just for a few hours. I told her I was taking some vacation time and could spend the whole week with her. She dozed again, and was happy when she woke up that I was still there.

***

The next day, I recounted for her the time she spent asleep. She couldn't believe she had slept for over four days. She proceeded to tell me the strangest story.

"For several nights before I went to sleep, two ladies and a man in a dark suit came and sat on the couch, across from my bed. They never spoke. They just watched me until I fell asleep. I wondered who they were, but was afraid to say anything to you because you might think I was going crazy. Then one night, they took my hand and together we left my room, assuring me it was all right. They took me to a place with huge doors which opened to a spacious entry area with walls made of gold. They took me to a bedroom, and told me I could go to bed, which I did because I was so tired."

"How did you get there?"

"I don't remember, but I thought I was only there one night. Several times a young girl with long blond hair, dressed in a white gown, came to talk to me. I think she was an angel. She told me it was okay to be there, and that I should rest. After a long nap, the angel came back and told me I could not stay any longer, that it was not my time. She said it was time to go home."

"Mother that was quite a dream."

"It was not a dream. I'm telling you that really happened."

She was positive she went to a waiting place for Heaven, and was watched over by an angel. Being told, "It was not her time," renewed her zest for life.

Did she cross over to Heaven?

***

One move thing I would like to share with you that happened last week. My granddaughter Hayley and her family were staying at our river home. Her husband, Stephen, was lying on our bed. (The one with Randall's underpants under it.) There is a clock radio on the bedside table. It came on for no reason. Stephen shut it off and checked to see if the alarm was set. It wasn't. It continued to come on several times, and he kept shutting it off. Stephen doesn't believe in mediums but he could not explain the things Mary was able to tell me.

While he lay on the bed, he felt a hand take hold of his ankle, and then heard Randall's voice say, "Stephen, Stephen." He is now a believer.

SEVENTEEN

As I started to write this book it was my intention to talk to other widows so I could share their experiences with my readers. As I met other women, we share our experiences, it was very comforting. At times you think you are all alone with the hurt inside. If you are a widow or widower, I hope this helps you during your time of grief.

***

My friend, Evelyn, introduced me to her neighbor, Camellia, who had lost her husband, Lorenzo, several years ago. She thought maybe Camellia needed someone to talk to who was grieving too. We made a date to meet at a local coffee shop to share our experiences.

Camellia was much younger than I, but when you lose your husband age doesn't matter. Loss of your spouse affects everyone differently. When I heard stories like Camellia's I realized how lucky I was to have fifty-eight years with Randall and was not left to raise my children alone. Camellia had a twenty-year-old son, and a fifteen year-old daughter who still lived at home when her husband died. Their emotions were all over the board.

As we chatted, I asked, "What was your early married life like?"

"We were in no hurry to have children. We both had great paying jobs, and a beautiful home in Beverly Hills. Lorenzo was from Italy and looked like a male model. He was six years older. Our life was fun and exciting. We attend a lot of social events and many cocktail parties.

"Several years later, in the 90s, we decided to start our family. We sold our house in Beverly Hills and left our high-society life behind. My mother lived in a small town, called Glendora. It was a town with families with young children. We decided to move close to my mother who lived alone. It was going to be nice to live close to her and she could enjoy her grand-children.

"After our first child, a boy, I became a stay-at-home mom. Later I became pregnant again. I thought that would be the perfect family. The oldest a boy and two years later a boy or a girl, but I lost the baby at eight weeks. Honestly, I thought that was the end of our family. A few years later I became pregnant again and had a little girl.

"Life was going pretty smoothly. Then in 2010, Lorenzo was having backaches. He had tolerated it for a year when he heard about City of Hope offering free clinical trials on stem cell transplants. He signed up for the trials, hoping for a cure. That was when he found out he had cancer, which meant weekly chemo trips to City of Hope. I went to all the treatments with him, and we would sit and talk about life for hours.

"During our talks, Lorenzo said to me, Once I'm gone, it's okay if you date your high-school sweetheart. That made me laugh. That was the farthest thing from my mind.

"In 2015 he started getting growths on his neck and back. Because of the chemo treatments they didn't want to operate on him, instead they started radiation. The chemo treatments stopped. He ended up with an anti-fungal infection in both lungs.

"He was sick for five years before he passed at the age of fifty-four. Even after the many talks that we had I was not ready when the time came for him to leave me. Although my two children and mother were around, I felt so alone. Lorenzo didn't have any family here, they all lived in Italy."

"Had you discussed how he wanted to be buried?" I asked.

"Yes, he wanted to be cremated. As difficult as it was, I made the arrangements for his Celebration of Life. When the service was over, I returned home and sat in his favorite chair like a zombie. Soon many friends came to the house to be with me and my family to offer their condolences. One of my friends had brought a chocolate cake. All I wanted to do was to sit in the chair and eat the cake. I was numb."

After everyone left, except for a few of Lorenzo's family members, his sister insisted that she take his ashes back with her to Italy where he could be laid to rest with his family. I objected. I wanted Lorenzo to stay with me. Her insistence became more than I could deal with. Having a total meltdown, I let him go.

"Everyone was gone, the house was quiet. As I sat in his chair, I thought, *He's really gone. Now what?* It took several days to process it all and recuperate. Not only from the loss of my loved one, but now, I had nothing to hold on to.

"I wasn't prepared for what I now had to deal with - paying bills, legal issues, all the credit cards that were in his name only. Decisions for the kids were difficult. I had no one to share or discuss issues with anymore. I was actually having a hard time functioning. I look back on it now, and I didn't deal with them well."

"How are the kids doing?" I asked.

"They are in denial. Losing their father and my loss affected each of us differently at different times. I wasn't much help as a single parent." She took a deep breath and continued. "I didn't know who to trust. I locked up everything. It's four years later, and I'm still fixing things."

"I know you're working now. Did you go to work right after Lorenzo's passing?" I asked.

"No. I hadn't worked in years. My house was paid for, and I had a savings, but didn't know how long that would last. Physically, I was falling apart. Since Lorenzo passed away, I have had three back surgeries followed by three weeks of vertigo. During all that, my mother passed away.

"Once I started feeling better, I decided to seek help from a medium. During that session, Lorenzo came through. He said he was sorry he wasn't here to help me but was proud of how I was handling everything. That experience seemed to give me some peace."

"It's been several years and you are still young. Have you thought about dating?" I asked.

"I wondered if there would ever be another man in my life. I tried Match.com and went on one dinner date. When the meal was over, he slipped the bill toward me!"

"What? What did you do?"

"I paid it and went on my merry way. No more dating sites for me."

***

Camellia and I still keep in touch. There still are days that are difficult for her.

She said she had a message for other widows: "You can't go over it, under it, or around it. You have to go through it. It takes time. Be patient with yourself. In the long run you will be stronger and wiser. Work on yourself. You need to recreate who you are. It's a second chance. Make life good! Accept help from friends and family. Embrace the change. Don't fight it."

EIGHTEEN

One of the ladies in my church asked me about my neighbor, Maggie, whose husband had recently passed away. Todd, Maggie's husband of twenty-four years of marriage, had died of cancer. Remembering how alone I felt after Randall passed away, I thought I should let her know she was not alone in her feelings. I decided to go by and visit with her.

Maggie opened the door. "Hi Tami."

"Just thought I'd stop by and check on you. How are you doing?"

"I don't know. Come in," she said. "Do you have time for a cup of coffee?"

"Sure, if it's already made."

"It is. I'm ready for another cup myself." She motioned for me to take a seat in the front room and returned shortly with cups for each of us.

"I knew it was coming," said Maggie, as she sat curled up in her husband's favorite chair. I could hear someone crying in one of the other rooms. I assumed it was her daughter Sherry.

"Now that he's really gone, I'm not ready." She continued, "I didn't realize how much I depended on him. He was such a gentle man. We were a true couple."

"I know just what you mean. I always thought I was pretty independent, but after Randall passed away it was all the little things he did I realize I missed and hadn't appreciated at the time."

"If you have been through this with a loved one, you know how demeaning cancer is," she said.

"I do know," I responded. "My father died of cancer at the age of sixty. The last twelve months I watched a six foot three man dwindle down to almost nothing."

"At night I'm so tired and think about going to bed, but I'd rather fall asleep in Todd's chair where his scent still is." She closed her eyes and the tears streamed down her cheeks. Periodically she broke into intervals of sobbing.

"You're tired. I'll come back another time."

"Don't mind me. I know I need to be strong for my daughter. I just feel so lost. I wonder what's ahead of me. I'm only fifty-one. What does the future hold for me and my daughter? Even though Sherry is here, I feel so alone."

"You need your rest," I said as I stood up to leave. "It's important you stay healthy."

"Thanks for coming by."

We hugged and I left.

***

"Mom! Mom!" said Sherry, touching her mother's arm. Maggie jumped when her daughter touched her. "It's two in the morning. Why don't you go to bed?"

"Wow, I must have fallen asleep," said Maggie, reaching out to hug her daughter. "We're going to be okay. We have each other."

"I thought I was prepared for Dad to go. He'd been sick for so long. But Mom, I'm not!"

"I know what you mean, honey. I thought I was ready too. We both have to be strong for each other. We are the only family we have here." She put her arm around her daughter and said, "Let's go to bed and see if we can sleep."

"Can I sleep with you tonight, Mom?" asked Sherry.

WHAT THE HELL JUST HAPPENED?

"Sure honey."

***

A week went by, and Sherry was back in school and Maggie was home alone. The days seemed so long. Friends would call or drop by but, once they left, the loneliness returned. Her friends could see she was sinking into depression, as they would tell her, "It just takes time to adjust. Time heals."

She wanted to yell back to them, "Easy for you to say. You don't know what it's like! I just miss him so much." She didn't realize how dependent she had been on him. He was so much help around the house. He even helped with the laundry and the cooking.

Sherry was spending more time away from home and hanging with her friends. Maggie was concerned. She had met some of Sherry's friends and was not happy with her choices. Maggie kept her thoughts to herself because she knew Sherry was still mourning and trying to keep her mind off the idea her dad was gone and would not be home at the end of the day.

The future scarred Maggie because she wasn't sure what was ahead. She hadn't worked for fifteen years. She was thankful her house was paid for, and there was the life insurance, but how long would that last?

***

Maggie stopped going to the gym. In fact, her exercise was minimal. She spent most of her time on the couch watching television. *I know I need to go back to the gym,* she told herself. *I need to pull myself together.* Her friends would ask her to go to dinner with them, but what fun was that? They were couples, and she was now a single woman. *Will there ever be another man in my life,* she wondered. *Or will it just be Sherry and me? I think it's lonely now, what will it be like when Sherry grows up, gets married, and maybe moves away? I'm not looking forward to when I'm totally alone. All my family is in Puerto Vallarta, Mexico. I sure would like to go see my sister, but I don't want to take Sherry out of school.*

***

One night at dinner, she told Sherry that she wanted to visit her sister during spring break. "I don't want to go," was Sherry's response. "Why can't I stay here? I could stay with my friend Lydia."

Maggie had met Lydia, and she was not one of Sherry's friends who she was concerned about. The next day, Sherry told her mother, "I talked with Lydia, and her mother after school and they said I could stay with them."

"Wait, we're getting a little ahead of ourselves. I haven't decided to go yet." *Maybe it would be good for her to get away from this house for while. Away from all the reminders,* thought Maggie.

"I'll give Lydia's mother a call and we'll see," she told Sherry. Lydia was an only child and her parents were divorced. Her mother said she welcomed Sherry to come and stay. Maggie called her sister, Diane, and made plans for the visit.

***

Diane was single. She liked to party and enjoyed the nightlife. The second night Maggie was there, Diane took her to her favorite nightspot. They had a few drinks, and Diane introduced her to some of her friends. She caught the eye of Tony, who was handsome, loved to dance, and was a few years younger than Maggie.

Todd had been gone for over a year, and the attention felt good. Maggie went home with him that night and spent the next few nights there. Tony was the total opposite of Todd. With him gone she was very lonely. After Todd died she wondered if another man would be attracted to her. Well, that question was now answered.

WHAT THE HELL JUST HAPPENED?

Tony asked her to move in with him. "Send for your daughter," said Tony. "I have plenty of room for her." She actually gave it a thought. *No, this is too quick!*

When she talked with her sister, she said, "Have you lost your mind?"

"I think so," said Maggie, "but just for a minute." She knew it was not love, it was a need. *It's time for me to go home.*

Tony took her to the airport and asked her to come back soon. She agreed but knew that was not in her future.

***

"So how was your visit, Mom?" asked Sherry, as they sat and had dinner.

"Diane is doing great. It was fun seeing her again," said Maggie. "And I met some of her friends. What was it like staying with Lydia?"

"I had a great time, and we went to a movie on Saturday night." That night, Maggie noticed for the first time she didn't hear Sherry crying herself to sleep.

Maggie didn't cry herself to sleep either. She questioned her action in Puerto Vallarta. *What was I thinking? I was just so lonely. I think it's time for me to find a job.*

***

Maggie returned to going to the gym, and found a job at the school district. Her and her daughter would go to a movie and out to dinner once a week. Maggie makes sure she finds time for her daughter. Yes, life is different now, but she has made some necessary adjustments to not let herself get depressed or feel sorry for herself.

NINETEEN

I would like to share with you some of my final thoughts.

First I must tell you I am not an attorney, and none of the following should be considered legal advice. It is just what I have personally experienced.

When I decided to write this book, my first thought was to let other widows know they are not alone in what they are experiencing and feeling. Then I changed my approach. If I can let women and men know what they might be facing when they lose a spouse, maybe I can help them be more prepared, which might make the loss less stressful.

The number one advice I would give a couple is to establish a Family Trust or Living Trust. Next time you receive an advertisement in the mail to attend a presentation for a Family Trust seminar, at least consider going and be informed. Then you can make the decision. Many times I've seen close-knit families fall apart, each fighting for what they think is right. If you leave written instructions on what you want after you are gone, and who gets what, the decision is made. Do yourself and your family a favor and make a Family Trust/Living Trust. This will also avoid your property going through probate, which is very expensive.

***

The following are after-the-fact items I experienced that you might avoid if you plan ahead:

At the time of a spouse's death, you will be asked how many death certificates you want. Many after death transactions will require an original death certificate. I suggest a minimum of twelve to fifteen. The certificates are less expensive if purchased at the time of death and easier to obtain. If a certificate is requested, ask if a copy would be acceptable. Never give out an original if you don't have to.

If you are the beneficiary of a pension or life insurance that is probably the first call you need to make. There will be documents to sign and an original death certificate will be required. If your spouse is collecting Social Security, an original death certificate will also be required. If you are both collecting Social Security, the survivor is eligible for the larger amount.

Make sure all vehicles and boat registrations are in both your names as or. Following one of the registered owner's death, transfer ownership into your name. Don't wait until you decide to sell the item. If it's not in your name it will cause additional difficulties.

Although I was the beneficiary on our investment portfolio, I found that task the most intense. If I hadn't been a businesswoman, I think I would have sat at my kitchen table and cried out of frustration. There was so much paperwork and documents to sign.

I recommend you leave the name and phone number of the contract agent on one of your investment statements. Once they are contacted about a death you will receive a multitude of documents. Before the documents are sent to you, ask the agent to highlight areas you need to initial or sign. If you have any questions, don't hesitate to call the agent or the documents will be returned to you for further signatures.

I didn't think it was important to change my house utilities into my name. Why should I? I was going to live here the rest of my life.

While I was having some work done on my patio, one of the workers broke the gas line that was hooked up to my barbeque. When I called the gas company to get it fixed, they informed me I was not on the account. This created some delays in the repair. I should have taken care of the name change earlier.

Having that happen, I proceeded to get my name changed on the Edison service as well. When I requested to have my account set-up on the equal monthly billing system, they told me they couldn't do it because I didn't have a track record.

"What? I've lived here for over forty years. What do you mean I don't have a track record?" They then explained that now I had a new account so there weren't any previous billings to average the monthly payment. Some things are so bizarre they aren't worth arguing about.

I was thankful that I managed all the bill paying. Randall would have been totally lost if I had been the first to go. Not only would he have not known some of the passwords or the answers to the security questions, i.e.; the name of my first dog or my father's middle name. It never seemed important enough to discuss with each other. We had a dear friend who lost his wife, who paid all their bills on-line. He didn't know where to start.

I suggest you make a list of the bills that are paid on-line with the passwords and answers to the security questions.

I paid all our credit card bills, and my name was on my card. Just because you pay the bill and your name is on your card does not mean you are the authorized cardholder.

One of the credit cards we used the most included travel miles. When I called to let them know Randall had passed away, the card was canceled. I lost all the benefits of the miles because I was not the authorized card holder.

The biggest disappointment, which I mentioned earlier, was our casino player card. We loved going to Las Vegas and combined our playing activities to accumulate more points. We had free hotel stays, free concerts, and other amenities.

I told you what happened in earlier chapters. They took my card away, and I haven't received any more invitations for free stays. As I wrote before, I showed them, I haven't been back!

Insurance policies need to be changed. I did take care of that right away; probably because my daughter works for an insurance agency. What would happen if I had a claim and hadn't changed the policy to my name? I can just imagine the problems I might have had.

Now is a good time to start a file on home repair companies. I didn't start one until Randall passed away. I started collecting mailers that I received on such companies.

Who would I call if the air conditioning went out? What would I do if my washing machine didn't work? What would I do if my electric garage door opener didn't work, and I had an appointment to get to? That did happen, and they came in a few hours. That file is like gold at times.

If your loved one selected cremation and you still want to have a traditional service, there are places where you can rent a casket.

***

I had managed a bank, a construction company, a care facility for developmentally disabled adults, an executive assistant to two companies' presidents, a lighting manufacturer and KB Home. I was confident that I could handle just about anything. I didn't realize how much I relied on my husband and took for granted that he would be around forever. So many things I didn't bother to learn related to the house, because Randall took care of them.

The first week after the funeral, I fell down the back steps. I didn't break anything, just bruised my ankle and walked with a limp for a few days. I didn't want my kids to know because they might think I can't take of myself or live alone. The next thing was my kitchen sink clogged up, but I had the number for Roto-rooter. That wasn't too upsetting.

My neighbor was having some yard work done, and one of the workers ran over my mailbox. Being a good neighbor, he replaced it the following day.

I had never done any gardening nor did I want too. We had a gardener who came once a week to mow the yard and do some light trimming. Randall did the major trimming and pruning of the four fruit trees we have in the backyard. We also have a small rose garden that he maintained. I just picked the beautiful roses for bouquets in the house.

Randall had set up about four sprinkler systems with timers. The timer for the front-yard was in our bedroom closet, of all places. I knew how to turn it off if it rained, but that's about it. There are three systems in the back yard that come on at different times of the day. Each system is a different brand. My son and the gardener couldn't figure out what system operated what. The yard was getting watered, so I guessed I should leave it alone.

The first winter I was alone I was taking care of my six-year-old great-granddaughter for a week. The heating system went out. I went to my file for house repairs and called a local serviceman. I couldn't get service for two days. The house was so very cold, but I had a gas fireplace, which took two people to light, safely. When Randall was here, I would hold the match and he would slowly turn on the gas. I was afraid to try it because I might blow up the house. For two days we stayed in our pajamas, wrapped in blankets, and watched cartoons. My great-grand-daughter thought that it was great fun.

The second summer the air-conditioner went out. My son-in-law gave me a number for a friend of his, and, thank goodness, I had service the next day. He also gave me a quick lesson on how to change the filter, and read the thermostat.

We also had a koi pond with a waterfall that Randall had built. I knew how to feed the fish, but that was all. The pond filter quit working and the waterfall stopped. The water wasn't looking too good and a few fish died.

I ordered a new filter, and my son-in-law installed it. I went to the place where Randall bought his fish and got a number for a pond-guy. He came and cleaned up the pond, and the fish were happy again.

The fish food was kept in a small locked wood box we had sitting by the pond. Randall told me to always keep the box locked. I thought that was to keep the grandkids from getting to the food and feeding the fishes too much. I knew they weren't coming over soon, so I didn't bother to lock the box. The next morning when I went to feed the fish, I found the wood box tipped over and the fish food container was gone. I looked around the yard and found the container. The lid was off, and it was empty. I knew we had raccoons and skunks. I guess they like fish food. I now keep the box locked and think of Randall every time I feed the fish.

Our house was the gathering place, and I wanted it to stay that way. Our family was getting bigger; not only in number but in size. It was getting a little crowded in the family room when we all got together. I thought maybe I would enclose the small patio area off our kitchen.

I contacted a contractor to discuss my plan to add on a room. Once we started talking, I realized that area would not make much difference. I now have a 400 square feet sunroom added to the back of my house. This was a great undertaking, and it took my mind off of being alone.

Of course, one thing led to another, and I added a stone planter and connected and replaced my two walkways with pavers.

One day the electrician came to hook up the power to the new sunroom. He asked, "Where is your electrical panel?"

"Hmmmmm?" I remembered seeing a metal box on the side of the house. "It's over here," I said with confidence. I showed him where the metal box was and was so proud that I hadn't embarrassed myself.

I feel simply lost most of the time, so I'm proud when I do little things I have never done before like putting the new license stickers on the license plate, taking out the trashcans for weekly pickup and the wheeling them back in place at the end of the day. The other day I even got out the screwdriver and tightened the toilet seat that was loose.

Randall had a vegetable garden every year. As I mentioned before, I don't do yard work. The first year he was gone, I just let the dirt sit there. Every time I walked by it, it made me sad. The second year, I bought some garden gloves. *Randall would be so proud of me*, I thought. *If I just planted a few tomato plants.* I went to Home Depot, walked around the garden department a few times, then got a cart and bought a few plants and some planter's soil. It came in such big bags I had to get a dolly to take it to the car. Before I left the cashier station I had one of the garden assistances take my picture standing next to the cart. I sent the picture to my children with the message, "Mom has her big girl pants on today!"

I was so proud of my garden as I watched it grow. I now understand why Randall found it so rewarding. I went back to Home Depot and bought some pots of flowers and placed them around my yard. It's amazing what a difference a pair of garden gloves makes.

Just a little word of advice, you can do it, or at least make yourself proud that you gave it a try.

I think keeping busy is important. It's so easy to find time for sadness and loneliness. Music made me sad at first, and one day I heard a song that made me happy. *What happened to me that I stopped listening to music?* I wondered. It's almost been four years, and I'm listening to music again, and sometimes I sing along.

Look for things that make you feel good. I know in the beginning you might think there aren't any.

I was talking with one of my widow friends who was having a bad day. "Why don't you go to the store and buy a new house plant or a few new colorful pillows for your couch," I told her.

She called me a few days later and thanked me for the advice. "I did buy a small potted plant for my kitchen window, and it helped the mood I was in," she said.

A year after Randall's passing, despite all the advice I have for others, I was feeling depressed. I knew I had to do something. I got in my car and went to the local bowling alley and joined a senior bowling league. Now I have a whole new group of friends, not to mention I'm getting a little exercise at the same time.

Don't forget about your health, and take a walk every day. Before Randall passed away, I was walking every morning. I knew it was important to keep that habit up. I'd be okay going, but when I was returning home, I would fall apart. He was always at the house waiting for me, and would ask, "How was your walk?" Knowing he wasn't going to be there ever again, I would cry all the way home. I usually went through four tissues. I knew I was getting better when I got down to only one.

How you decide to deal with your grief is up to you. Everyone handles it differently. You lived one journey with your spouse, now you are on your own journey. The choice is yours, make it a good one.

***

I am now on my own journey. Where it will take me, I have no idea. Everyday something happens or I see a picture that reminds me of the wonderful life we had together. Yes, there were some bad times, but why dwell on them. What difference does it make now? I still miss him every day.

You are welcome to email me with your questions or comments or just to talk. I might not have the answer, but together we can work it out. (tamgram40@gmail.com)

TWENTY

The following pages are worksheets for your use:

Personal Contacts:

Family: Name   Phone No.

           _____   _____
           _____   _____
           _____   _____
           _____   _____

Friends: _____   _____
           _____   _____
           _____   _____
           _____   _____

Clergy: _____   _____
Attorney: _____   _____
Doctor: _____   _____

WHAT THE HELL JUST HAPPENED?

Dentist: _____ _____
Pharmacy: _____ _____
Insurance: _____ _____
            _____ _____

Here are some things you might be asked:

Full Legal Name: _____
Date of Birth: _____
Place of Birth: _____
Parents Name: _____
Siblings: _____ _____
          _____ _____
          _____ _____

Places where you have lived: _____
                              _____

Military service: _____
Church affiliation: _____
Education: _____
Occupation: _____
Employment: _____
             _____

Marriage: Date: _____   Spouses Name: _____

Awards & Notable accomplishments: _____
_____

Notes: _____
_____
_____
_____

Bank Accounts:
    Name of Bank: _____
        Address: _____
        Type: Ck/Sav _____
    Name of Bank: _____
        Address: _____

Investments: (Stocks, Bonds, 401K, Pension, Mutual Funds, IRAs

    Description: _____
        Type: _____
        Account No: _____
        Contact/Phone: _____
    Description: _____
        Type: _____
        Account No: _____
        Contact/Phone: _____
    Description: _____
        Type: _____
        Account No: _____
        Contact/Phone: _____

WHAT THE HELL JUST HAPPENED?

Insurance Policies: (Home, Autos, Health, Life, Long Term, Other)

Type: _____
Company: _____
Agent: _____
    Phone No: _____
Policy No. _____

Type: _____
Company: _____
Agent: _____
    Phone No: _____
Policy No. _____

Type: _____
Company: _____
Agent: _____
    Phone No: _____
Policy No. _____

Type: _____
Company: _____
Agent: _____
    Phone No: _____
Policy No. _____

Mortgage:

    Lender Name:_____

    Address: _____

    Account No: _____

Auto:

    Make: _____

    Loan with _____

    Account No: _____

    Make: _____

    Loan with _____

    Account No: _____

Boats/Motor Home:

    Type: _____   Make: _____

    Lender: _____

    Account No: _____

    Type: _____   Make: _____

    Lender: _____

    Account No: _____

WHAT THE HELL JUST HAPPENED?

Credit Cards:

Type: _____ Account No: _____

Type: _____ Account No: _____

Type: _____ Account No: _____

Type: _____ Account No: _____

Type: _____ Account No: _____

Websites:

Name: _____ Password: _____

Name: _____ Password: _____

Name: _____ Password: _____

Name: _____ Password: _____

Name: _____ Password: _____

Name: _____ Password: _____

Name: _____ Password: _____

Other accounts/Subscriptions

Name: _____ Password: _____

Name: _____ Password: _____

Name: _____ Password: _____

Name: _____ Password: _____

Name: _____ Password: _____

www.ingramcontent.com/pod-product-compliance
Lightning Source LLC
Chambersburg PA
CBHW021448070526
44577CB00002B/307